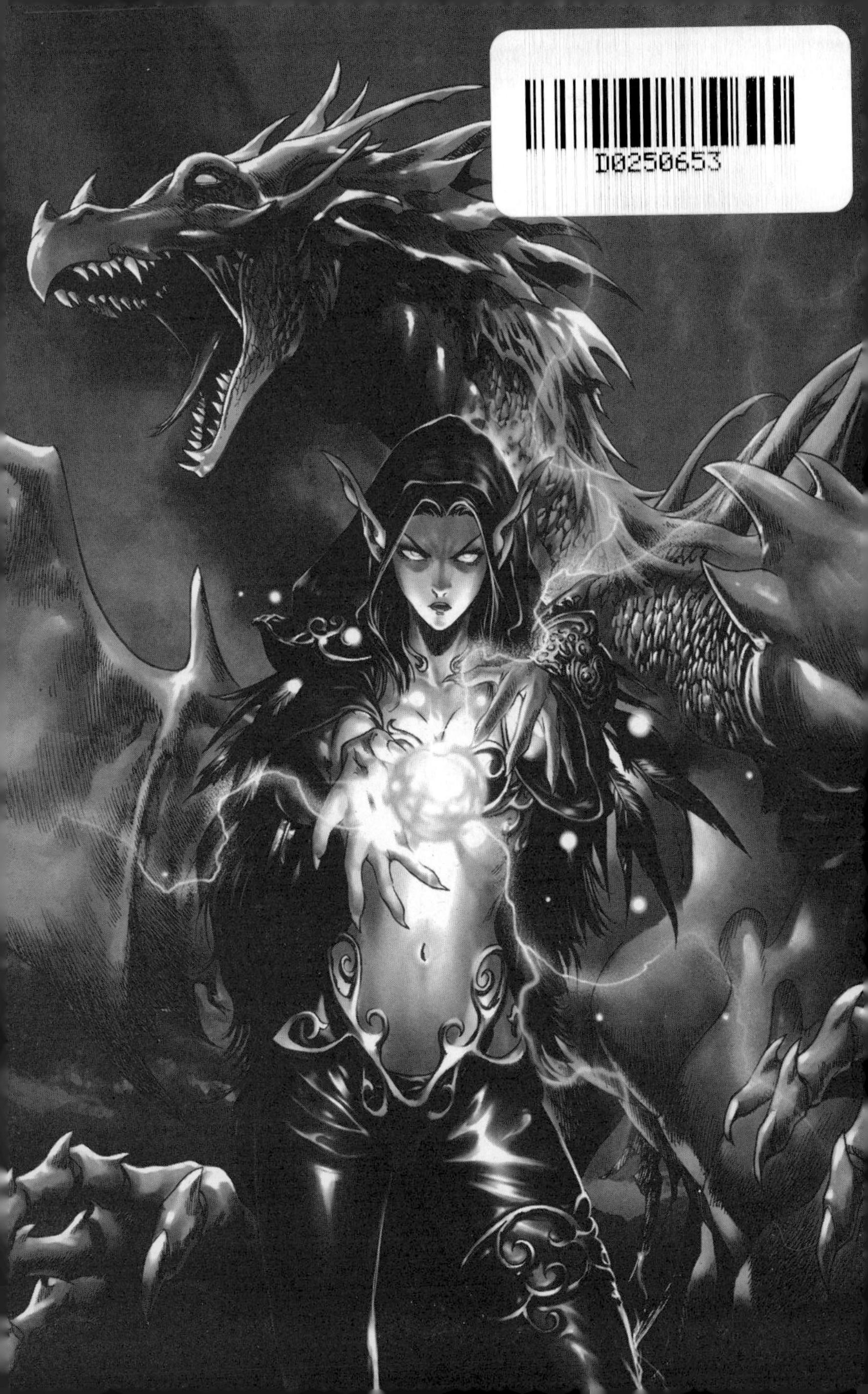

Warcraft®: The Sunwell Trilogy™ Vol. 3
Written by Richard A. Knaak
Illustrated by Jae-Hwan Kim

Lettering and Layout - Rob Steen
Production Artist - Lucas Rivera
Cover Artist - Jae-Hwan Kim
Cover Design - James Lee

Editor - Rob Tokar
Digital Imaging Manager - Chris Buford
Pre-Production Supervisor - Erika Terriquez
Art Director - Anne Marie Horne
Production Manager - Elisabeth Brizzi
Managing Editor - Vy Nguyen
Editor-in-Chief - Rob Tokar
VP of Production - Ron Klamert
Publisher - Mike Kiley
President and C.O.O. - John Parker
C.E.O. and Chief Creative Officer - Stuart Levy

A **TOKYOPOP** Manga

TOKYOPOP and 🐾 are trademarks or registered trademarks of TOKYOPOP Inc.

TOKYOPOP Inc.
5900 Wilshire Blvd. Suite 2000
Los Angeles, CA 90036

E-mail: info@TOKYOPOP.com
Come visit us online at www.TOKYOPOP.com

Special thanks to Chris Metzen, Lisa Pearce, Cory Jones, Brian Hsieh, Gloria Soto, and Matt Kassan.

ISBN: 978-1-59532-714-7

First TOKYOPOP printing: March 2007
10 9 8 7 6 5 4 3 2 1
Printed in the USA

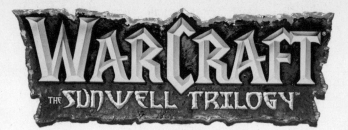

WARCRAFT®
THE SUNWELL TRILOGY™

VOLUME 3

GHOSTLANDS

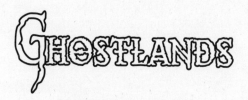

WRITTEN BY
RICHARD A. KNAAK

ILLUSTRATED BY
JAE-HWAN KIM

TOKYOPOP®

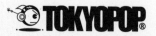

HAMBURG // LONDON // LOS ANGELES // TOKYO

HISTORY OF THE WORLD OF

The world of Azeroth has long been plagued by the misuse of magic. Originally, only dragons and night elves were able to practice the mystic arts, though eventually even humans began to wield the unstable energy. Unfortunately, the unrestrained spell-casting eventually caught the attention of a malevolent, extra-dimensional force known as the Burning Legion.

The Burning Legion's first attempt to invade Azeroth, known as the War of the Ancients, was only thwarted after many lives were lost and the world's sole continent was shattered. With their second attempt, the Burning Legion used the orcs from the world of Draenor as their pawns.

Twisted and corrupted by the Burning Legion's influence, the orcs invaded Azeroth through the Dark Portal. After many ferocious battles, this Second War ended with the orcs' defeat and imprisonment. Still determined to conquer Azeroth, the Burning Legion created one of its most twisted servants, the Lich King, to weaken Azeroth's defenders.

The Lich King spread a plague of death and terror across Azeroth that was meant to snuff out human civilization. All those who died from the dreaded plague would arise as the undead, and their spirits would be bound to the Lich King's iron will forever.

The army of the dead swept across the land, and Quel'Thalas, the glorious homeland of the high elves which had stood for thousands of years, was no more. The undead Scourge then moved south to Dalaran, and then to Kalimdor, home of the night elves.

Though the undead Scourge was stopped at Kalimdor, they had essentially transformed Lordaeron and Quel'Thalas into toxic Plaguelands. Grieving for the loss of their homeland, most of the high elves have adopted a new name and a new mission. Calling themselves blood elves, they now seek out and siphon magic from any available source, including demons.

Meanwhile, half of the undead forces staged a coup for control over the undead empire. Eventually, the banshee Sylvanas Windrunner and her rebel undead--known as the Forsaken--claimed the ruined capital city of Lordaeron as their own and vowed to drive the Scourge from the land.

Currently the Lich King resides in Northrend; he is rumored to be rebuilding the citadel of Icecrown. His trusted lieutenant, Kel'Thuzad, commands the Scourge in the Plaguelands. Sylvanas and her rebel Forsaken hold only the Tirisfal Glades, a small portion of the war-torn kingdom, while the humans, orcs, and night elves are trying to rebuild their societies.

WARCRAFT
THE SUNWELL TRILOGY

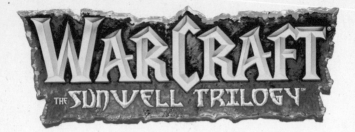

The story thus far...

The Sunwell was a pool of mystical energy that was the essence of the high elves' lives. Located in the elven city of Quel'Thalas, this source of magic was as important to the elves as eating or breathing. They used its vast power to build their cities, mold the landscape and make whatever they desired. Unfortunately, Dar'Khan was a high elf who desired much more than the rest of his brethren, leading him to an unholy pact with Arthas, the corrupted human knight who would later become the Lich King.

Dar'Khan enabled the undead Scourge to bypass Quel'Thalas' fabled defenses while he drained the Sunwell's energies. While his proud home was overrun by vicious, zombified corpses, and Dar'Khan fought his fellow elven sorcerers for control of the well, something went horribly wrong. The Sunwell's power exploded spectacularly, ravaging what little remained untouched by the Scourge. Dar'Khan was saved by the power of his dark lord, and sent across the continent in search of the Sunwell's escaped magic...though he was not alone in his quest.

MALYGOS, LORD OF THE BLUE DRAGONFLIGHT, COMMANDED YOUNG KALECGOS TO INVESTIGATE A STRANGE SURGE OF MAGICAL POWER. HOWEVER, BEFORE HE COULD REACH HIS DESTINATION, KALEC WAS SHOT DOWN BY A MOTLEY BAND OF DRAGON HUNTERS LED BY HARKYN GRYMSTONE.

ASSUMING THE FORM OF A HALF-ELF TO ESCAPE THE HUNTERS' NETS, A WOUNDED KALEC WAS AIDED BY ANVEENA, A KIND, INNOCENT MAIDEN WHO LIVED NEARBY. KALEC TRIED TO WARN ANVEENA AWAY, BUT SHE SEEMED UNCONCERNED ABOUT THE PURSUING HUNTERS. EVEN MORE REMARKABLY, THE YOUNG WOMAN SEEMED UNFAZED BY KALEC'S TRUE NATURE, THOUGH MOST PEOPLE'S REACTION TO MEETING A DRAGON WOULD BE TO FLEE OR TRY TO KILL IT.

STILL ON THE RUN FROM GRYMSTONE'S BAND, KALEC AND ANVEENA FOUND ANVEENA'S HOME REDUCED TO BURNING WRECKAGE BY DAR'KHAN, WHO PLACED PAIN-INDUCING MYSTICAL COLLARS AROUND THEIR NECKS TO FORCE THEM TO REVEAL ALL THEY KNEW ABOUT THE SUNWELL.

DAR'KHAN TRIED TORTURING KALEC FOR INFORMATION, BUT HE WAS INTERRUPTED BY THE ARRIVAL OF TYRYGOSA, A FEMALE BLUE DRAGON WHO IS ALSO

Kalecgos
A young blue dragon. Though trapped in humanoid form by a mystical collar Dar'Khan placed around his neck, Kalec retains many of his magical talents, including the ability to create a sword out of nothingness.

KALEC'S INTENDED. TOGETHER, TYRI AND KALEC MANAGED TO WIPE OUT DAR'KHAN'S UNDEAD SERVANTS AND DRIVE THE ELF AWAY...BUT THEY COULD NOT REMOVE THE COLLARS HE HAD PLACED ON HIS TWO CAPTIVES.

SIFTING THROUGH THE SHATTERED TIMBERS OF ANVEENA'S HOME IN SEARCH OF HER PARENTS, THE TRIO INSTEAD DISCOVERED A STRANGE EGG, WHICH HOUSED AN EVEN STRANGER WINGED SERPENT. ANVEENA NAMED HIM RAAC (FOR THE NOISE HE MAKES) AND KALEC AND TYRI SUSPECTED THAT THE BIZARRE CREATURE MIGHT HAVE SOMETHING TO DO WITH THE SUNWELL ENERGY THAT HAD DRAWN THE ATTENTION OF THE BLUE DRAGONFLIGHT AND DAR'KHAN.

SINCE KALEC'S COLLAR PREVENTED HIM FROM TRANSFORMING, TYRI CARRIED HER COMPANIONS TO THE TOWN OF TARREN MILL IN SEARCH OF BOREL, A MAN

Anveena
A caring, innocent young maiden. Anveena helped a wounded Kalecgos escape from dragon hunters, though her home and parents were destroyed.

WHOM ANVEENA'S PARENTS HAD
SPOKEN OF OFTEN. THOUGH SHE HAD
NEVER MET HIM, SHE BELIEVED HE
MIGHT BE ABLE TO HELP THEM REMOVE
DAR'KHAN'S COLLARS. THE GROUP
ATTRACTED A LOT OF ATTENTION IN
THE SMALL TOWN, INCLUDING THAT OF
PALADIN JORAD MACE.

AT TARREN MILL, GRYMSTONE HAD
THE DRAGONS CORNERED WHEN HE
SUDDENLY FOUND THAT HE AND HIS
BAND WERE SURROUNDED BY THE
UNDEAD SCOURGE AND DAR'KHAN.
DAR'KHAN REVEALED THAT HE HAD
DISGUISED HIMSELF AS A HUMAN
PRINCE TO PROVIDE THE VENGEFUL
DWARF WITH THE RESOURCES NEEDED
TO KILL ANY DRAGONS THAT MIGHT
BE DRAWN TO THE AREA BY THE
SUNWELL'S POWER. AS DAR'KHAN

Tyrygosa
A female blue dragon and Kalec's
intended. When forced to assume a
humanoid shape, she refuses to look
merely human. In her words, "At least
elves are aesthetically pleasing."

PREPARED TO TAKE RAAC FROM ANVEENA, A SURPRISE
ATTACK FROM JORAD MACE HELPED THE DRAGONS AND
DRAGON HUNTERS TURN THE TIDE.

WITH THEIR COMBINED EFFORTS, THE UNDEAD WERE
WIPED OUT AND DAR'KHAN WAS CONSUMED IN A BLAST OF
TYRI'S DRAGON FIRE. WHEN MACE INFORMED THE OTHERS
THAT THEY MIGHT FIND BOREL ON AERIE PEAK, AN
APOLOGETIC HARKYN GRYMSTONE ADVISED THEM TO SEEK
HIS COUSIN, LOGGI, WHO RESIDED IN THE MOUNTAINS NEAR
THERE.

HOPING THAT LOGGI MIGHT BE ABLE TO REMOVE THE
MAGICAL COLLARS, KALEC, ANVEENA, TYRI, RAAC AND
JORAD MACE SEARCHED NOT ONLY FOR THE DWARF, BUT
ALSO FOR THE MYSTERIOUS BOREL. THOUGH THEY

Jorad Mace

A human paladin whose loyalty was sworn to Arthas...before Arthas betrayed his father, his homeland and his species. Mace is continually haunted by his terrible loss.

EVENTUALLY FOUND LOGGI AT AERIE PEAK, THEY ALSO ENDED UP IN THE MIDDLE OF A WAR BETWEEN THE UNDEAD ICHOR AND THE FORSAKEN BARON MORDIS. MORDIS TRIED TO SACRIFICE ANVEENA TO DEFEAT ICHOR, ONLY TO BE DESTROYED HIMSELF ALONG WITH HIS UNDEAD OPPONENT. IN THE MIDST OF THE MELEE, KALEC WAS RESCUED FROM A POTENTIALLY FATAL FALL BY A MYSTERIOUS FORCE THAT SEEMED TO EMANATE FROM ANVEENA. THE SURPRISES ONLY MOUNTED AS THE SUPPOSEDLY DEAD DAR'KHAN SUDDENLY RE-APPEARED, KILLED LOGGI AND KIDNAPPED ANVEENA.

AND NOW--WITH ONLY THE QUESTIONABLE GUIDANCE OF RAAC TO AID THEM--KALEC, JORAD, AND TYRI MUST GIVE CHASE. THE TERRIBLE CHILL FILLING THE YOUNG BLUE'S BEING IS NOT FROM THE BATTLE IN THE SNOW, BUT RATHER BECAUSE HE FEARS HE KNOWS JUST WHERE THE MURDEROUS RENEGADE IS TAKING ANVEENA...

CHAPTER ONE
THE NIGHTMARE PLAINS

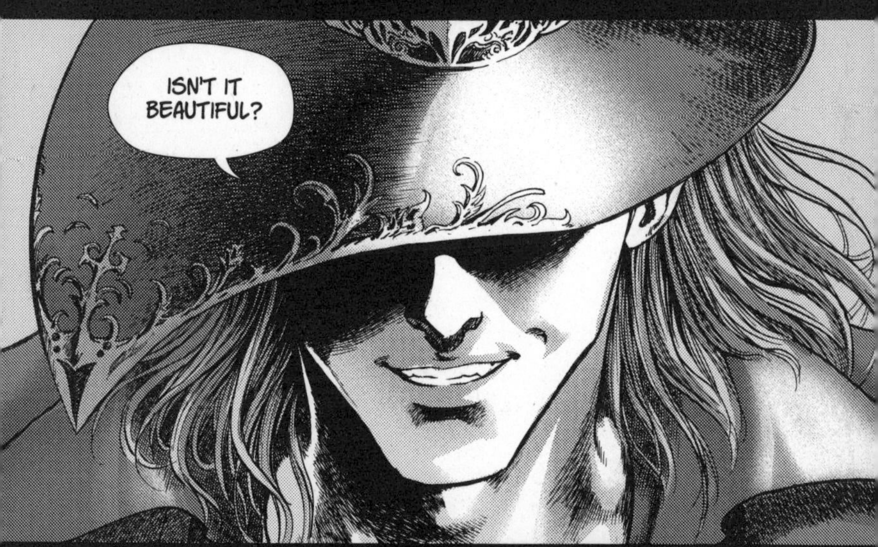

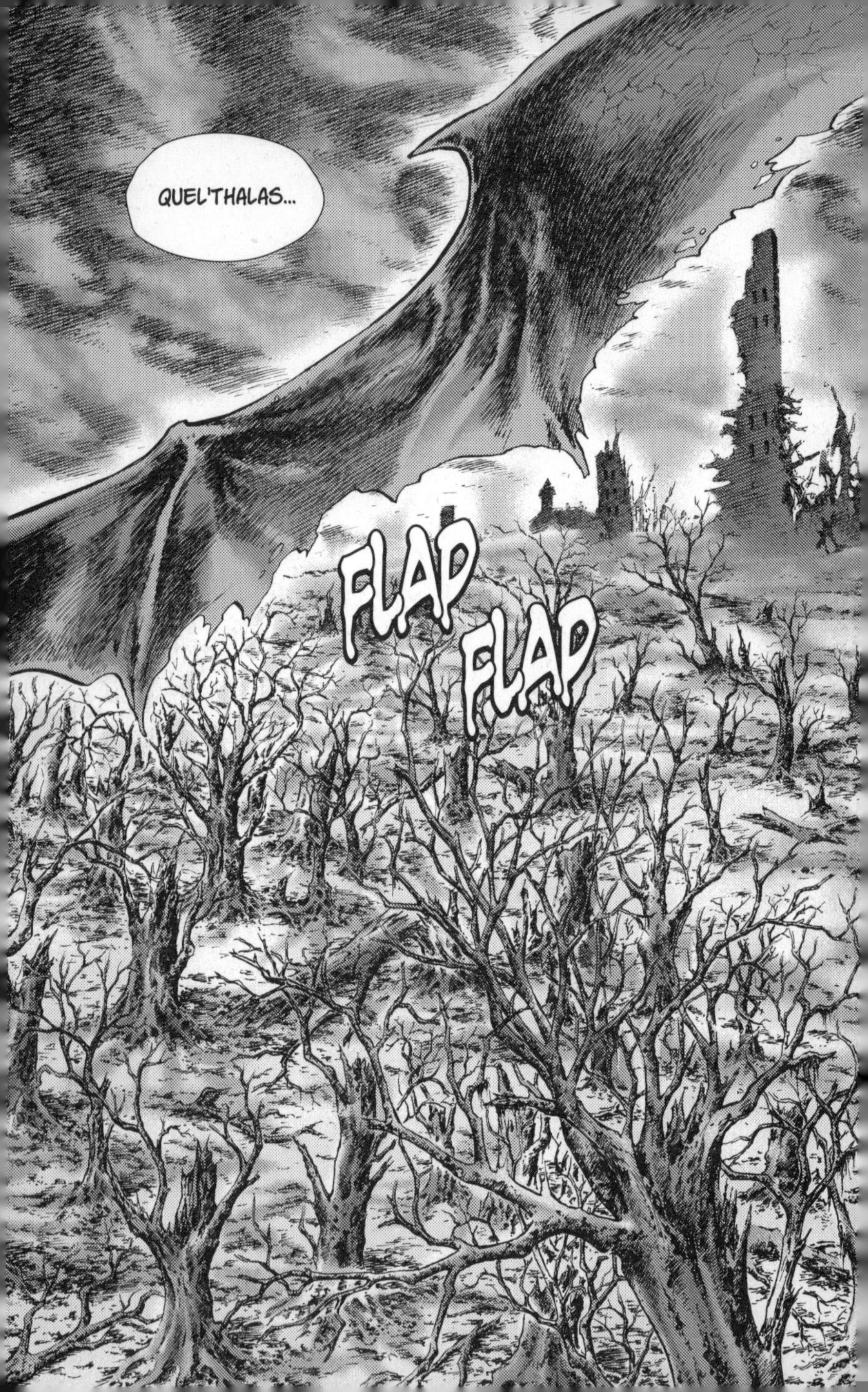
QUEL'THALAS...
FLAP
FLAP

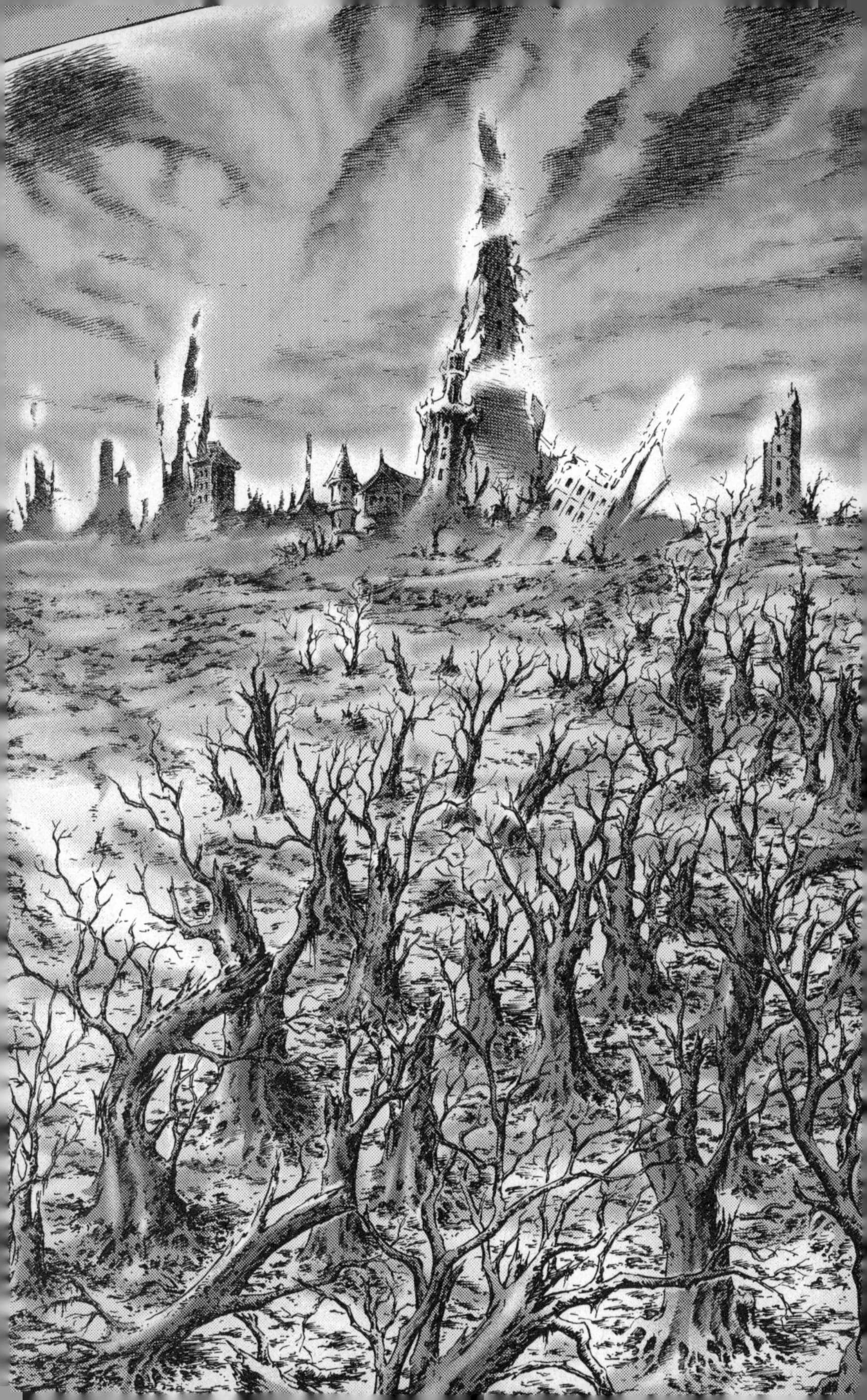

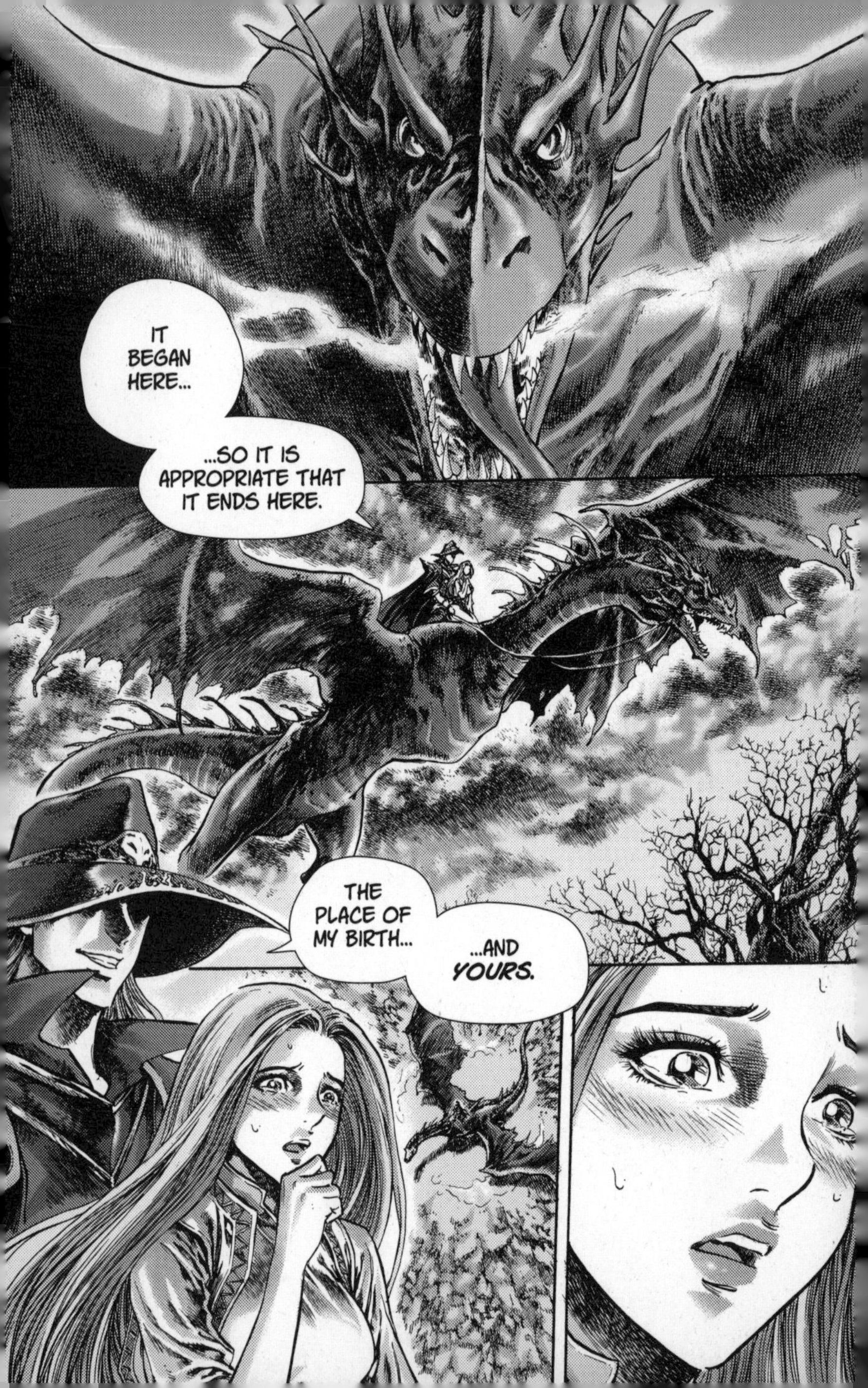
IT BEGAN HERE...
...SO IT IS APPROPRIATE THAT IT ENDS HERE.
THE PLACE OF MY BIRTH...
...AND *YOURS.*

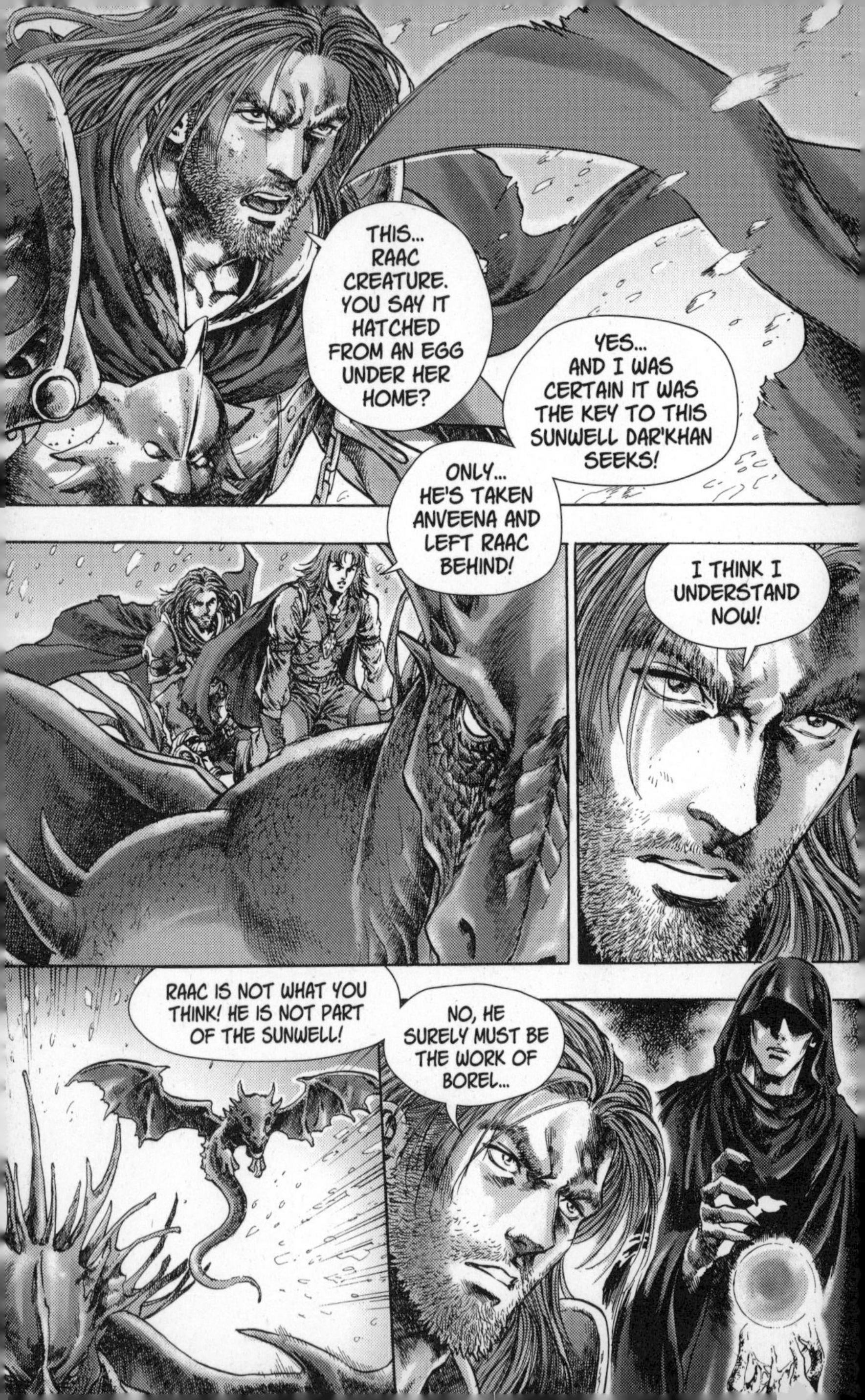
THIS... RAAC CREATURE. YOU SAY IT HATCHED FROM AN EGG UNDER HER HOME?
YES... AND I WAS CERTAIN IT WAS THE KEY TO THIS SUNWELL DAR'KHAN SEEKS!
ONLY... HE'S TAKEN ANVEENA AND LEFT RAAC BEHIND!
I THINK I UNDERSTAND NOW!
RAAC IS NOT WHAT YOU THINK! HE IS NOT PART OF THE SUNWELL!
NO, HE SURELY MUST BE THE WORK OF BOREL...

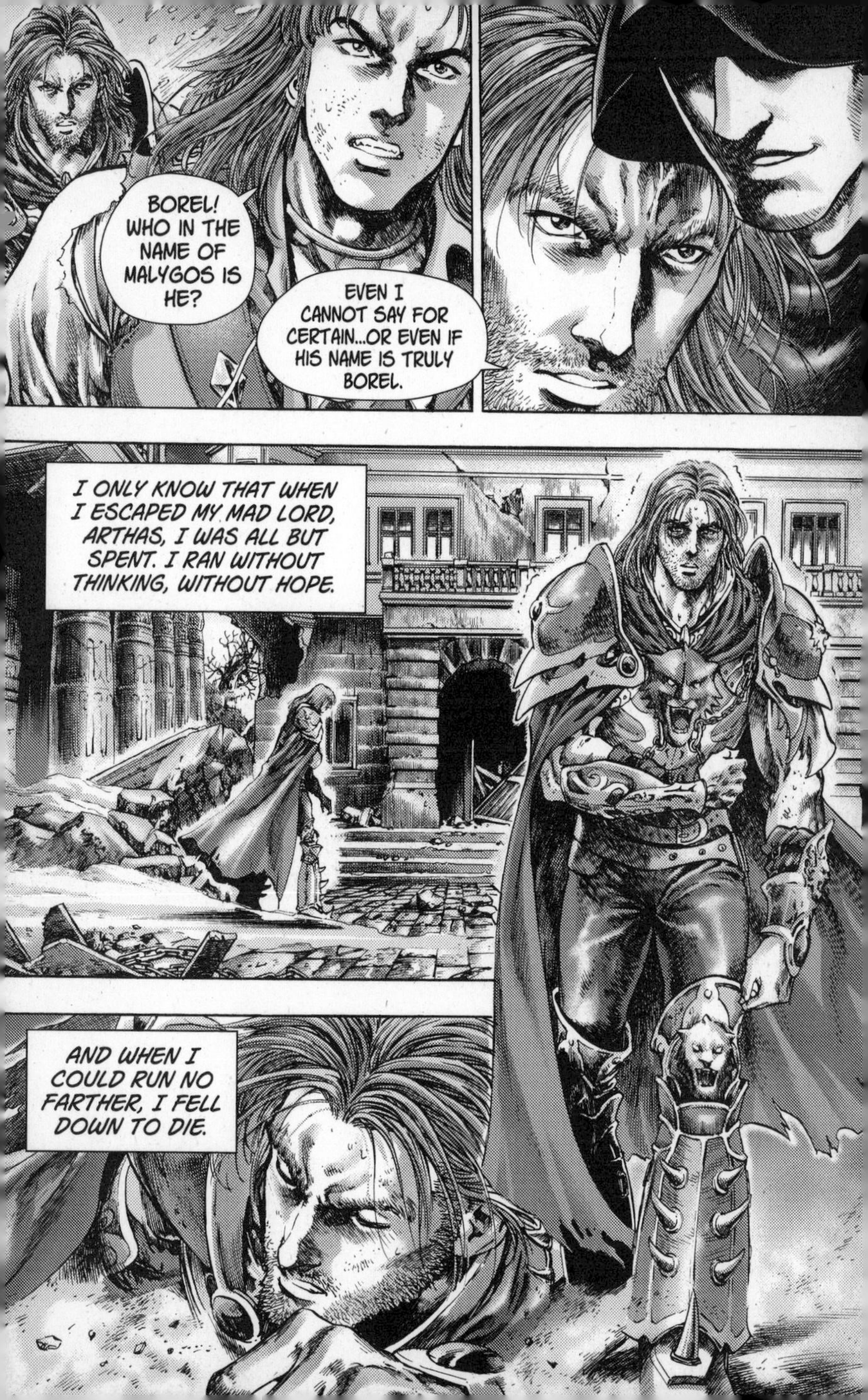
BOREL! WHO IN THE NAME OF MALYGOS IS HE?
EVEN I CANNOT SAY FOR CERTAIN...OR EVEN IF HIS NAME IS TRULY BOREL.
I ONLY KNOW THAT WHEN I ESCAPED MY MAD LORD, ARTHAS, I WAS ALL BUT SPENT. I RAN WITHOUT THINKING, WITHOUT HOPE.
AND WHEN I COULD RUN NO FARTHER, I FELL DOWN TO DIE.

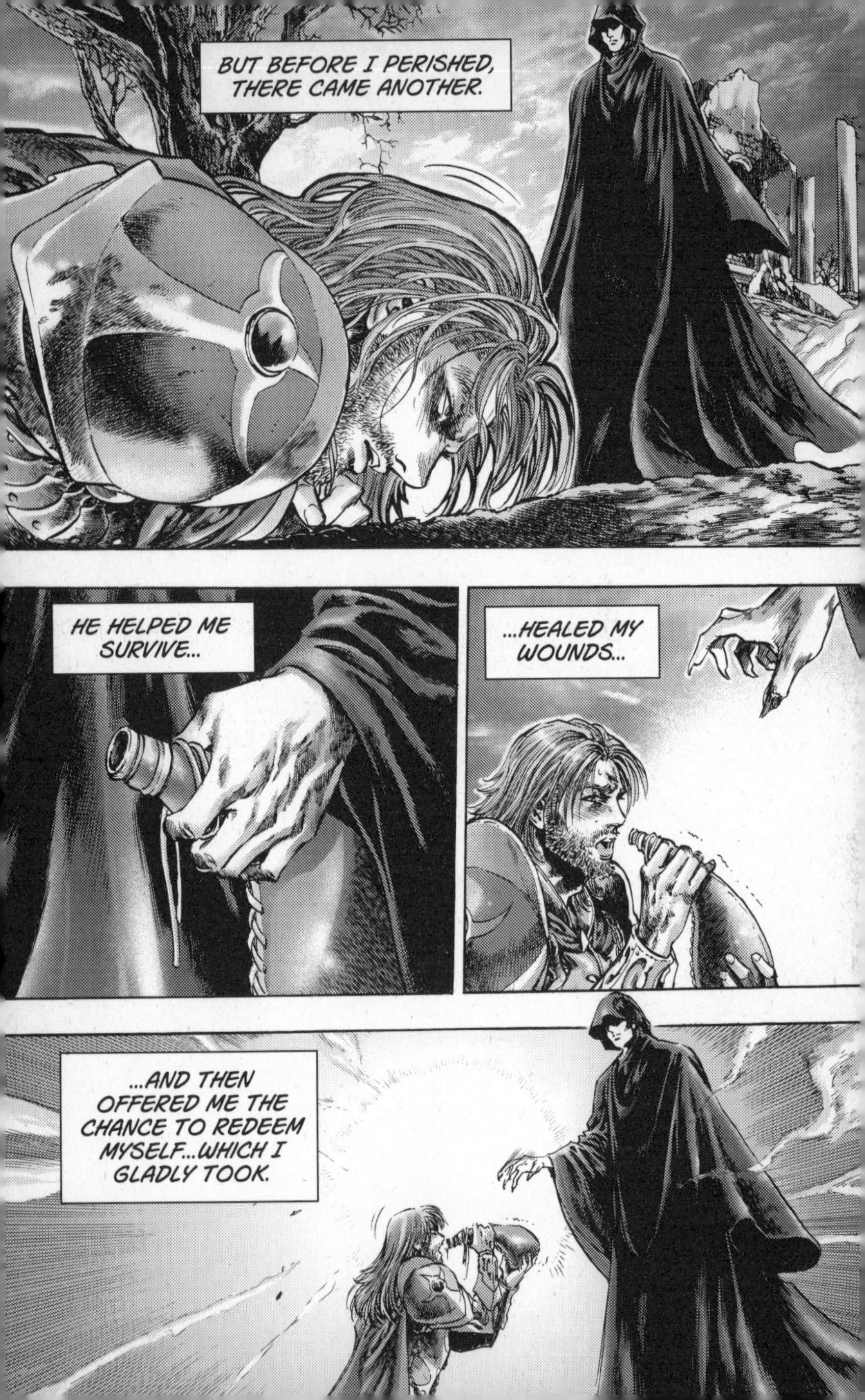
BUT BEFORE I PERISHED, THERE CAME ANOTHER.
HE HELPED ME SURVIVE...
...HEALED MY WOUNDS...
...AND THEN OFFERED ME THE CHANCE TO REDEEM MYSELF...WHICH I GLADLY TOOK.

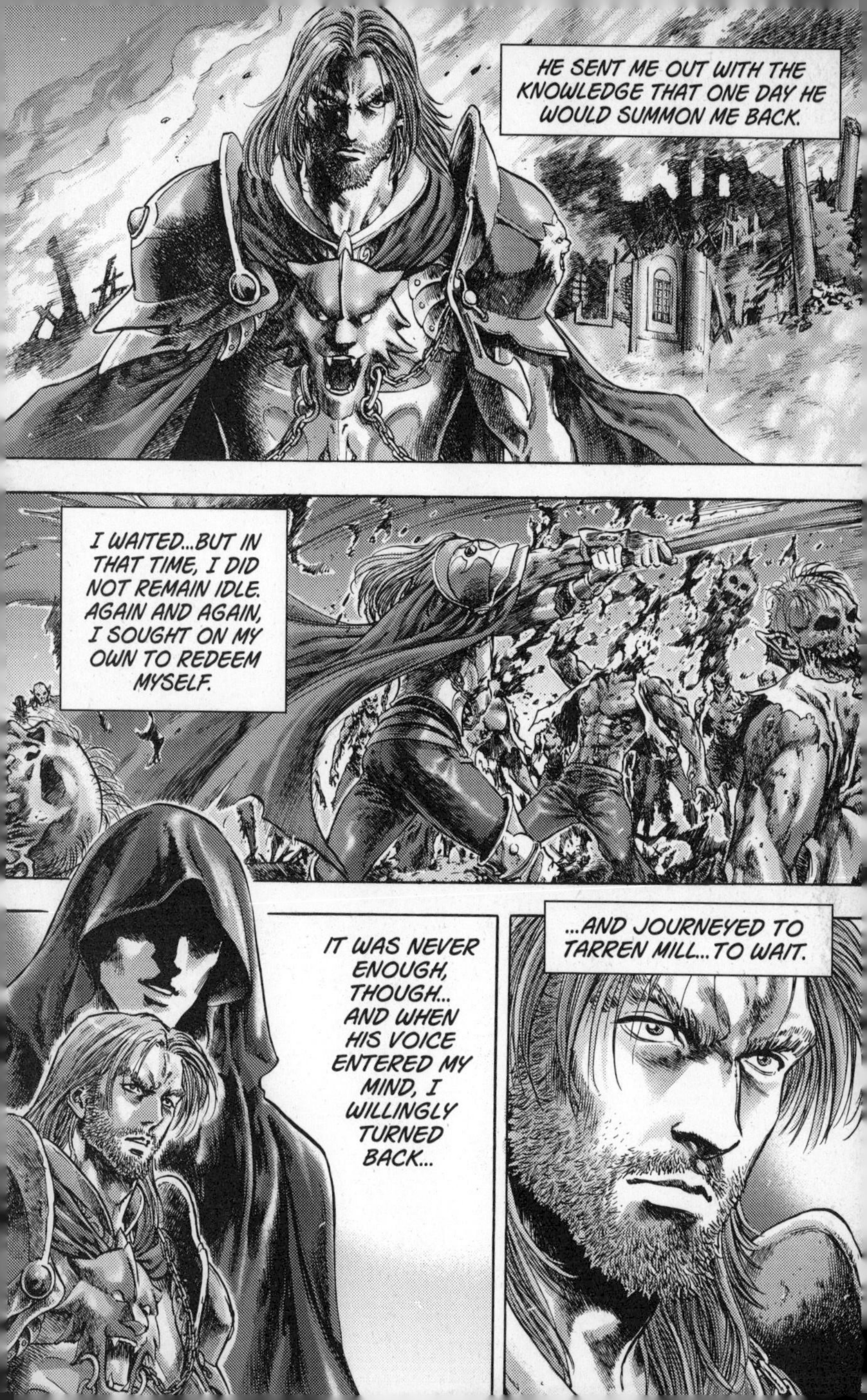
HE SENT ME OUT WITH THE KNOWLEDGE THAT ONE DAY HE WOULD SUMMON ME BACK.
I WAITED...BUT IN THAT TIME, I DID NOT REMAIN IDLE. AGAIN AND AGAIN, I SOUGHT ON MY OWN TO REDEEM MYSELF.
IT WAS NEVER ENOUGH, THOUGH... AND WHEN HIS VOICE ENTERED MY MIND, I WILLINGLY TURNED BACK...
...AND JOURNEYED TO TARREN MILL...TO WAIT.

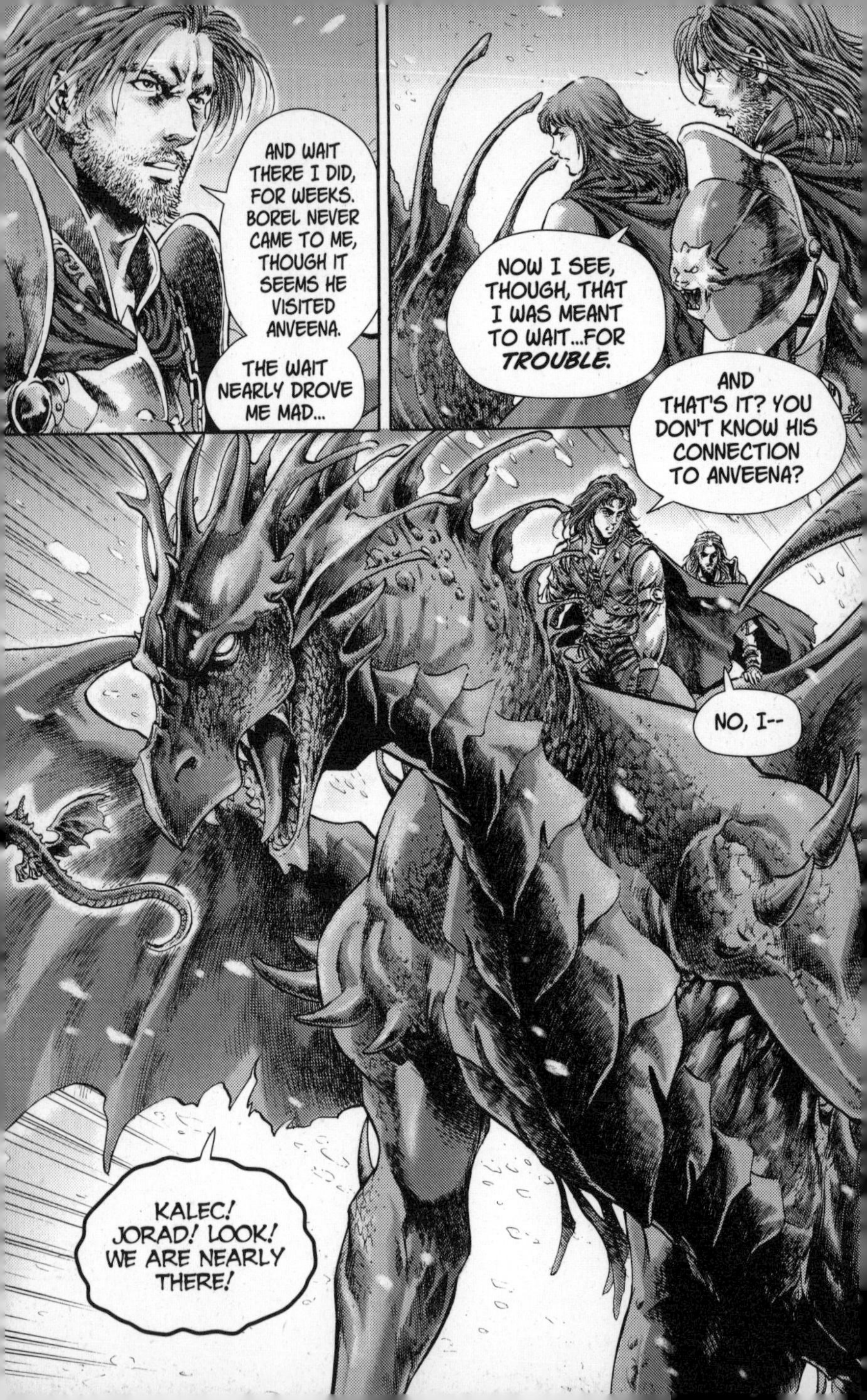
AND WAIT THERE I DID, FOR WEEKS. BOREL NEVER CAME TO ME, THOUGH IT SEEMS HE VISITED ANVEENA.
THE WAIT NEARLY DROVE ME MAD...
NOW I SEE, THOUGH, THAT I WAS MEANT TO WAIT...FOR *TROUBLE.*
AND THAT'S IT? YOU DON'T KNOW HIS CONNECTION TO ANVEENA?
NO, I--
KALEC! JORAD! LOOK! WE ARE NEARLY THERE!

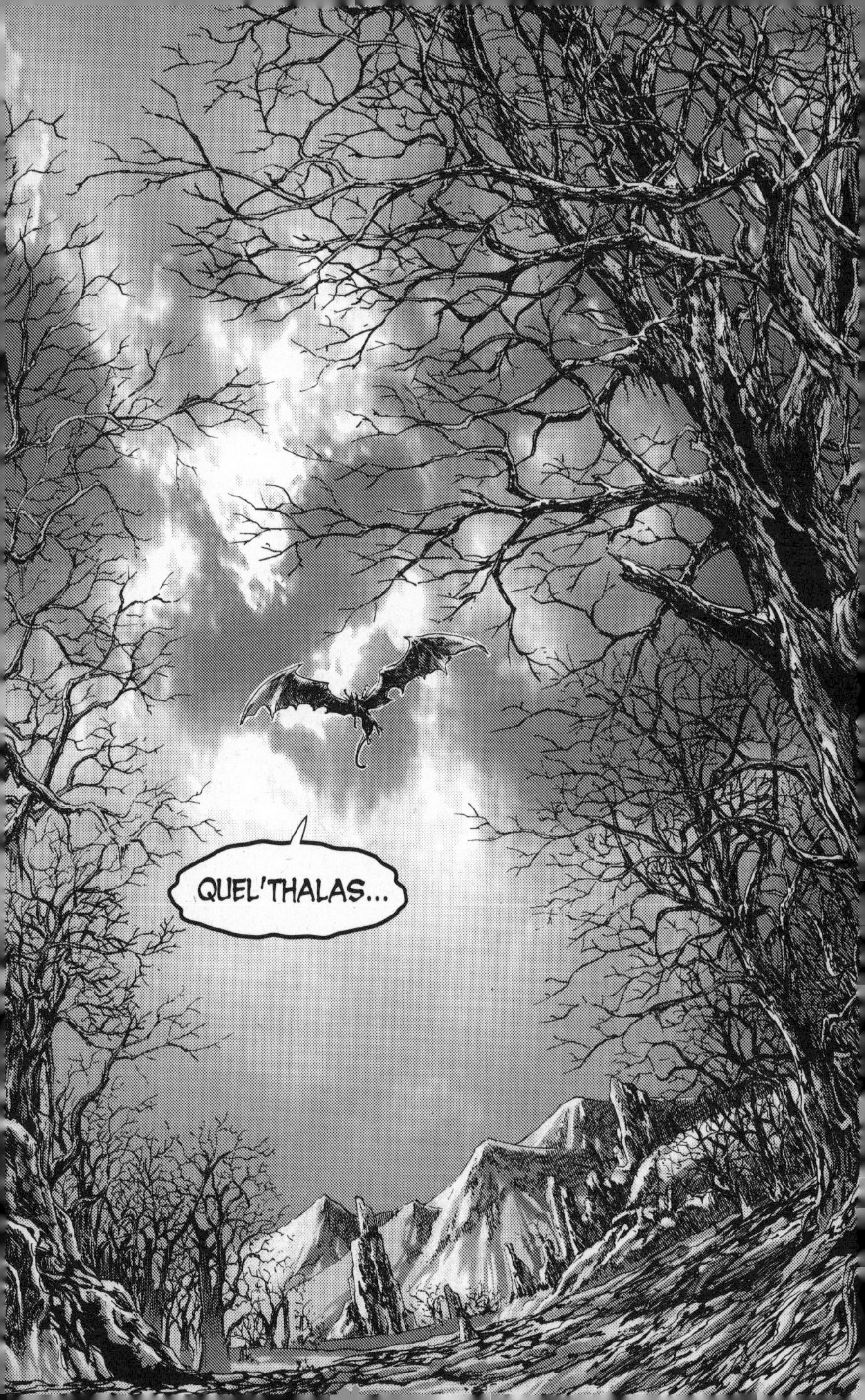
QUEL'THALAS...

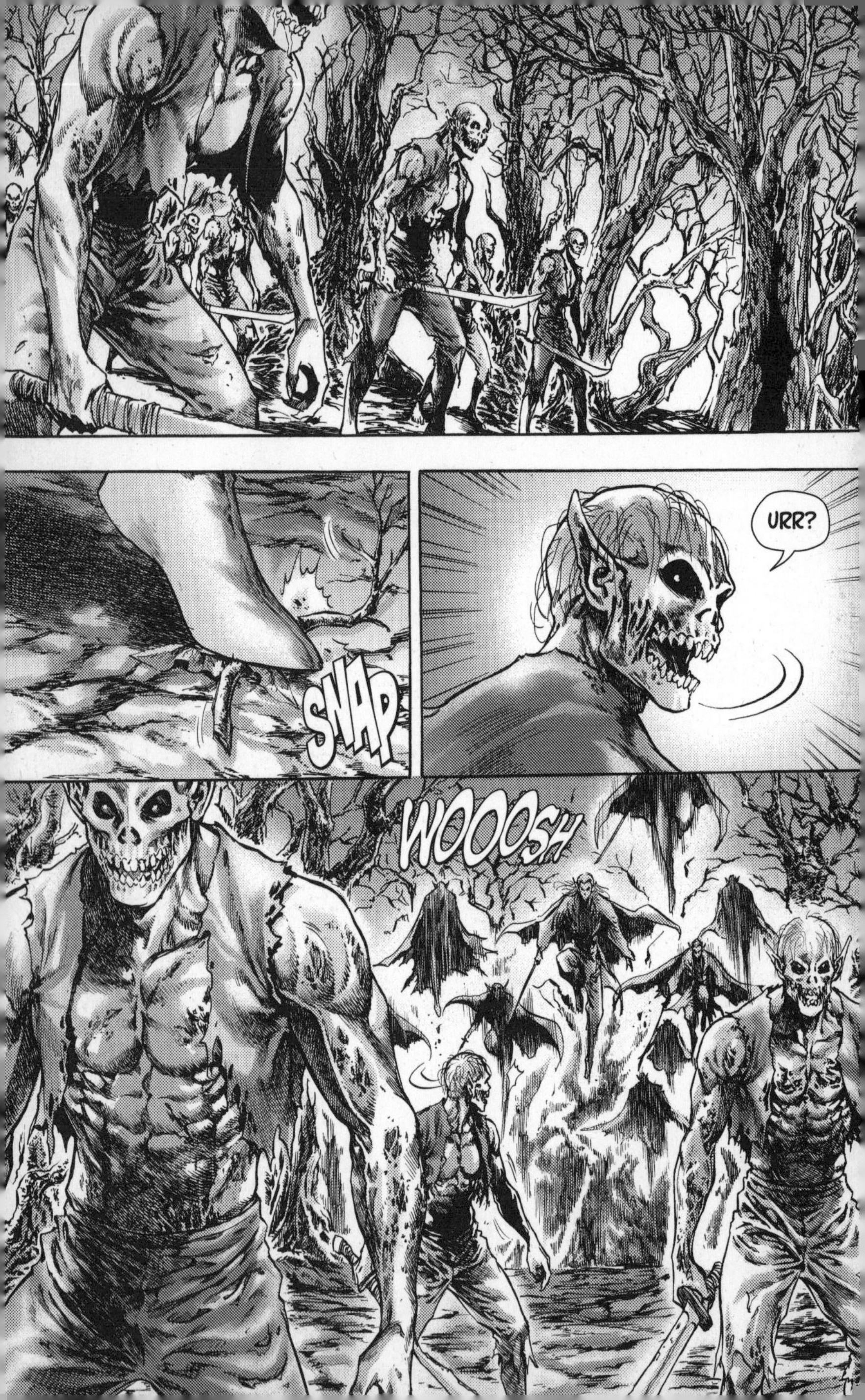

SNAP
URR?
WOOOSH

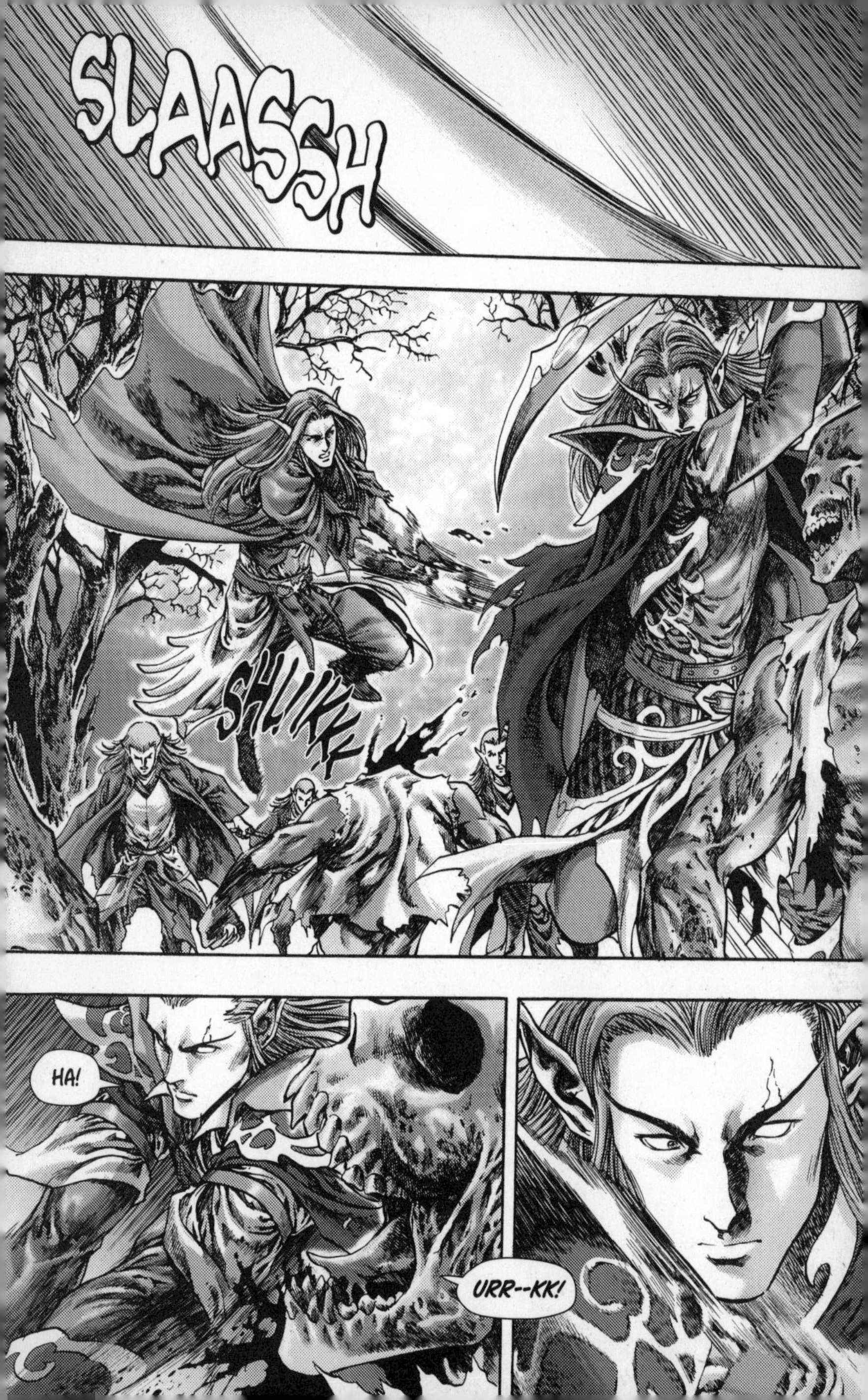
SLAASSH
SHIKKK
HA!
URR--KK!

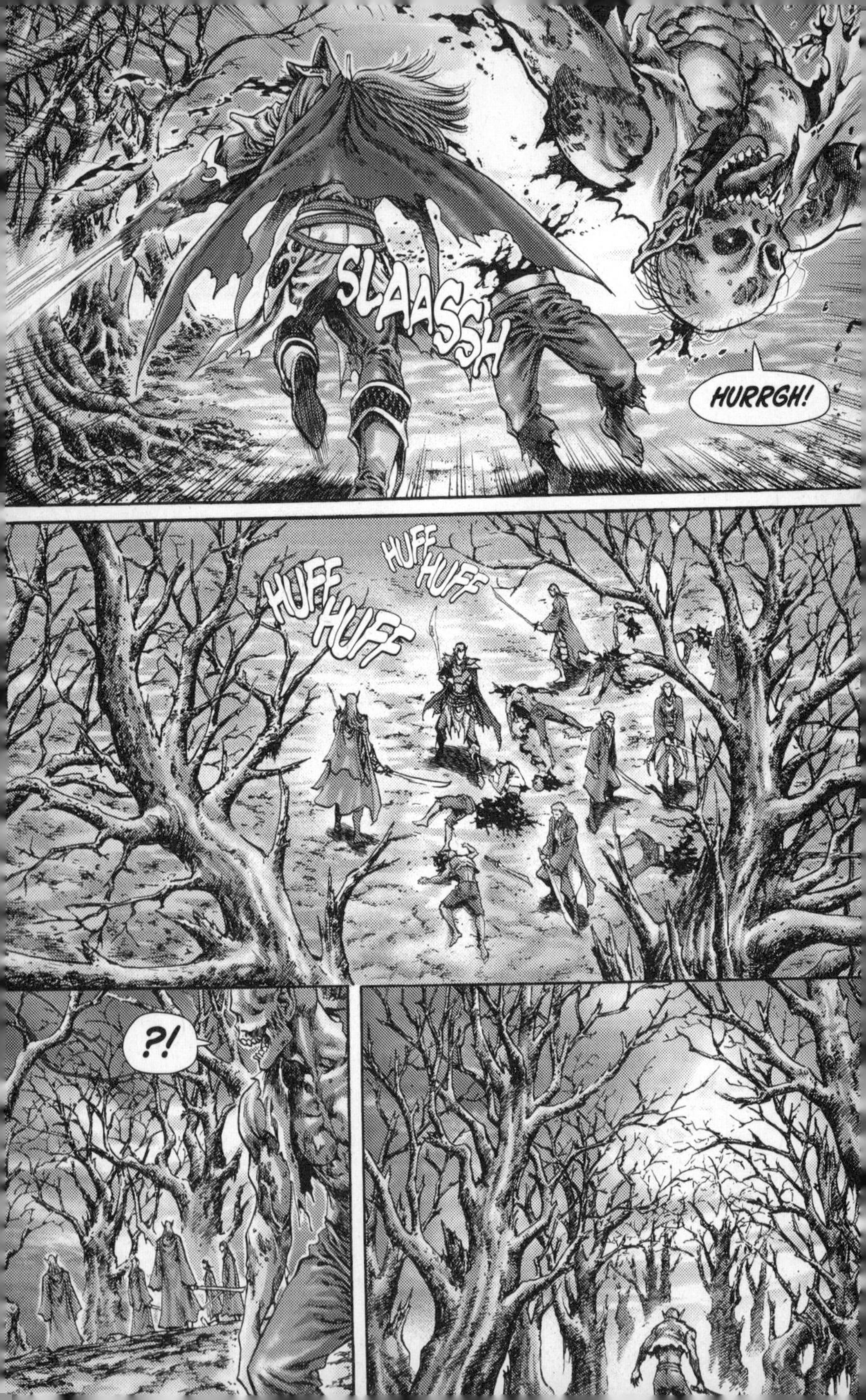
SLAASSH
HURRGH!
HUFF HUFF
HUFF HUFF
?!

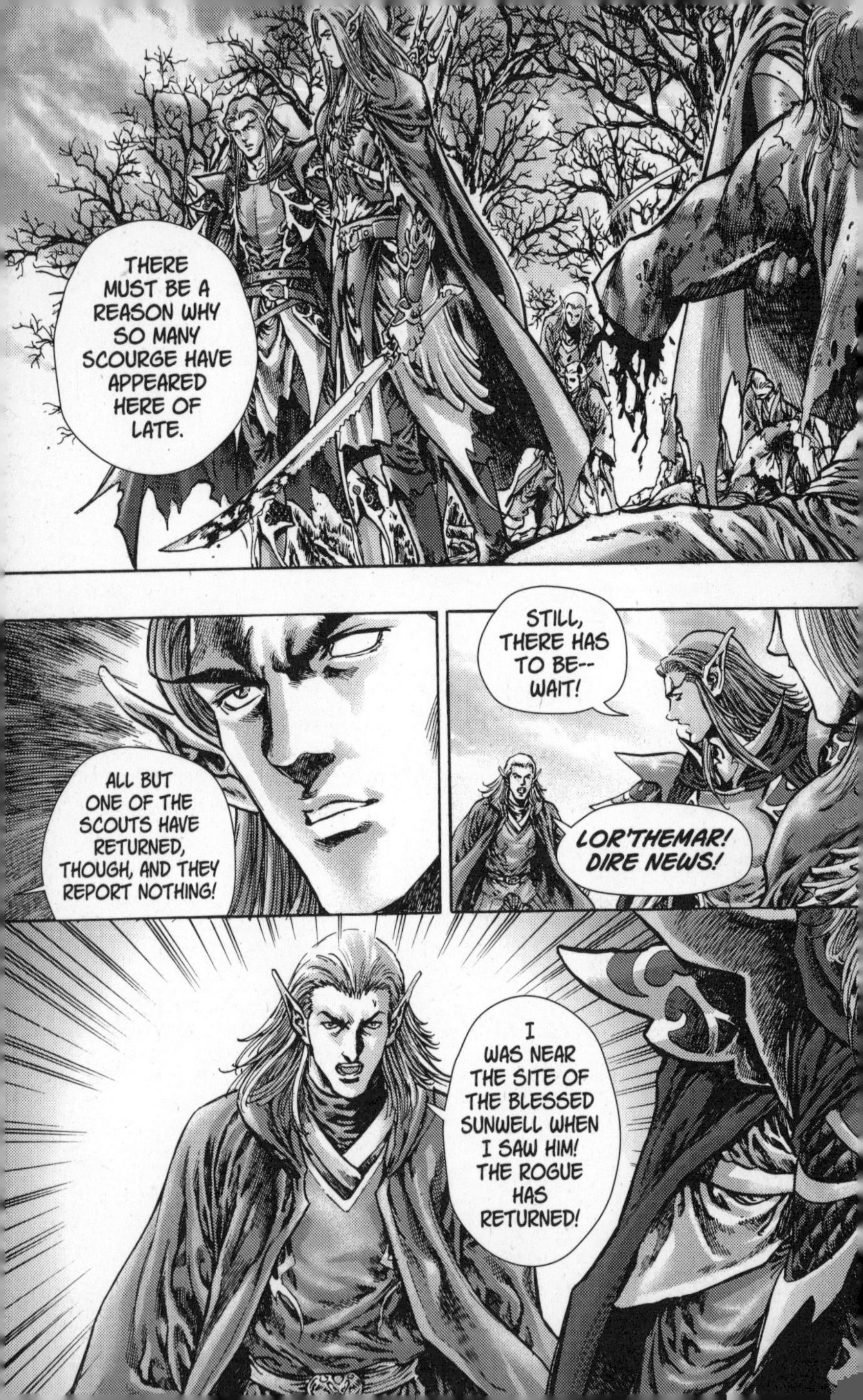
THERE MUST BE A REASON WHY SO MANY SCOURGE HAVE APPEARED HERE OF LATE.
ALL BUT ONE OF THE SCOUTS HAVE RETURNED, THOUGH, AND THEY REPORT NOTHING!
STILL, THERE HAS TO BE-- WAIT!
LOR'THEMAR! DIRE NEWS!
I WAS NEAR THE SITE OF THE BLESSED SUNWELL WHEN I SAW HIM! THE ROGUE HAS RETURNED!

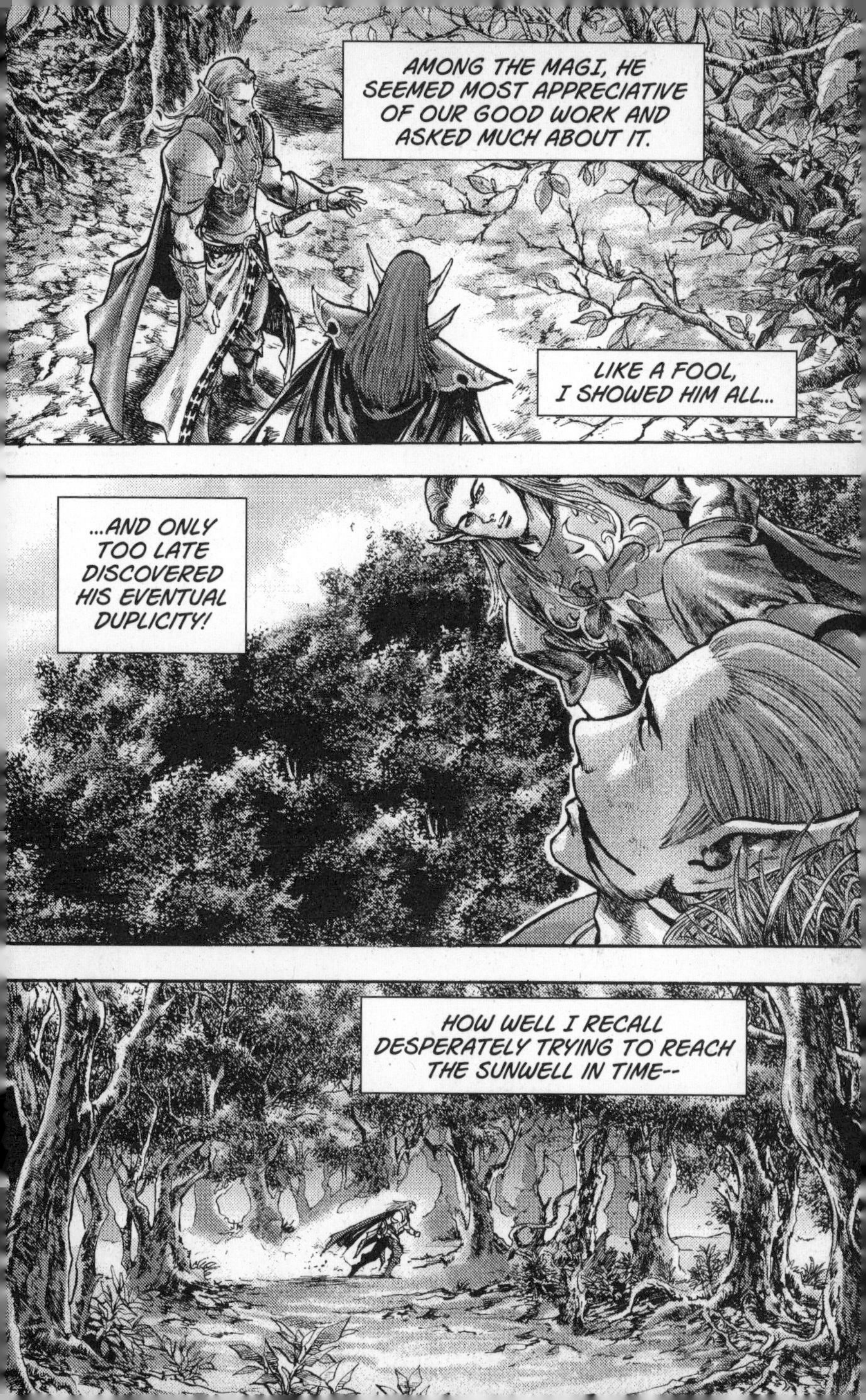
AMONG THE MAGI, HE SEEMED MOST APPRECIATIVE OF OUR GOOD WORK AND ASKED MUCH ABOUT IT.
LIKE A FOOL, I SHOWED HIM ALL...
...AND ONLY TOO LATE DISCOVERED HIS EVENTUAL DUPLICITY!
HOW WELL I RECALL DESPERATELY TRYING TO REACH THE SUNWELL IN TIME--

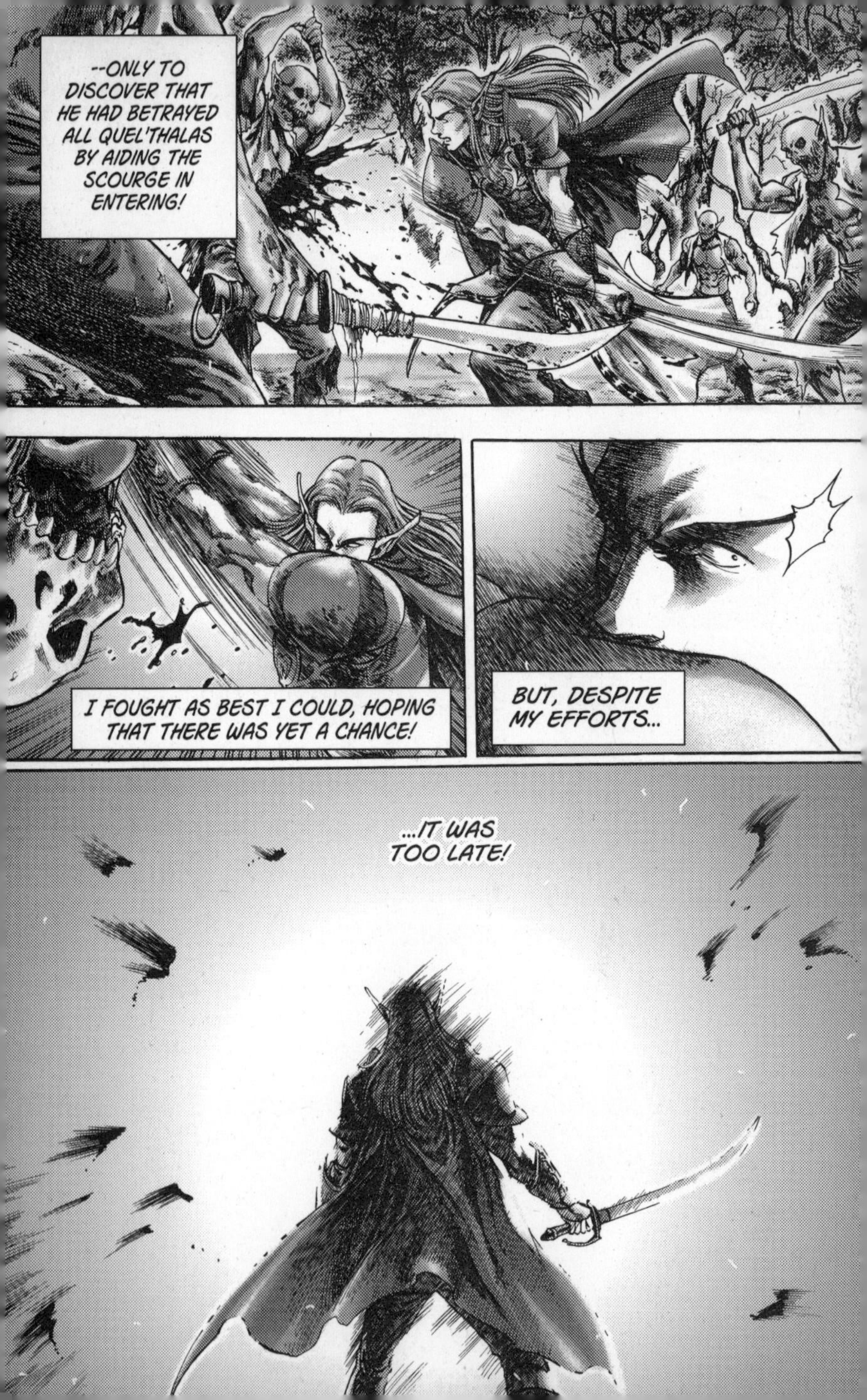
--ONLY TO DISCOVER THAT HE HAD BETRAYED ALL QUEL'THALAS BY AIDING THE SCOURGE IN ENTERING!
I FOUGHT AS BEST I COULD, HOPING THAT THERE WAS YET A CHANCE!
BUT, DESPITE MY EFFORTS...
...IT WAS TOO LATE!

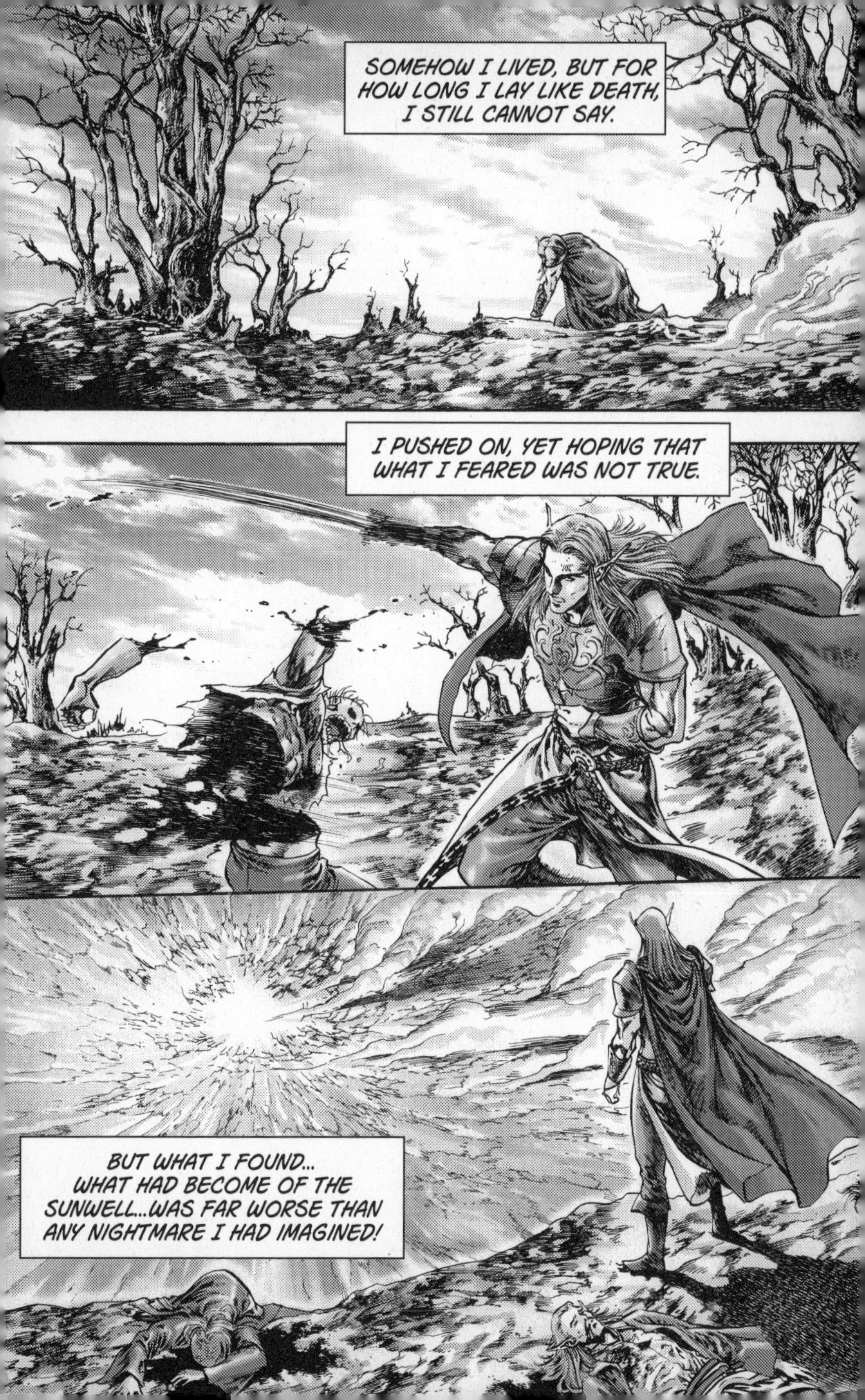
SOMEHOW I LIVED, BUT FOR HOW LONG I LAY LIKE DEATH, I STILL CANNOT SAY.
I PUSHED ON, YET HOPING THAT WHAT I FEARED WAS NOT TRUE.
BUT WHAT I FOUND... WHAT HAD BECOME OF THE SUNWELL...WAS FAR WORSE THAN ANY NIGHTMARE I HAD IMAGINED!

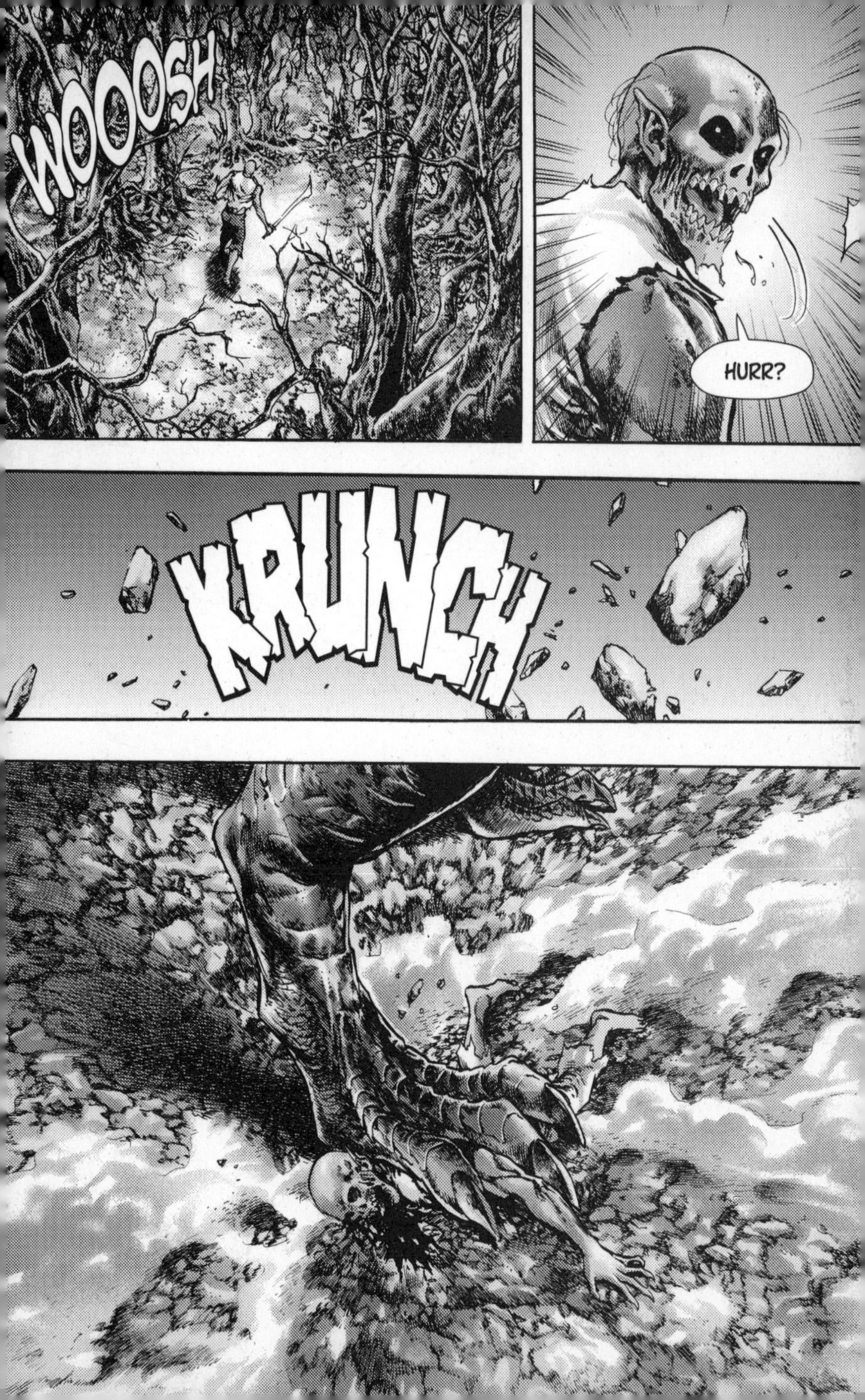
WOOOSH
HURR?
KRUNCH

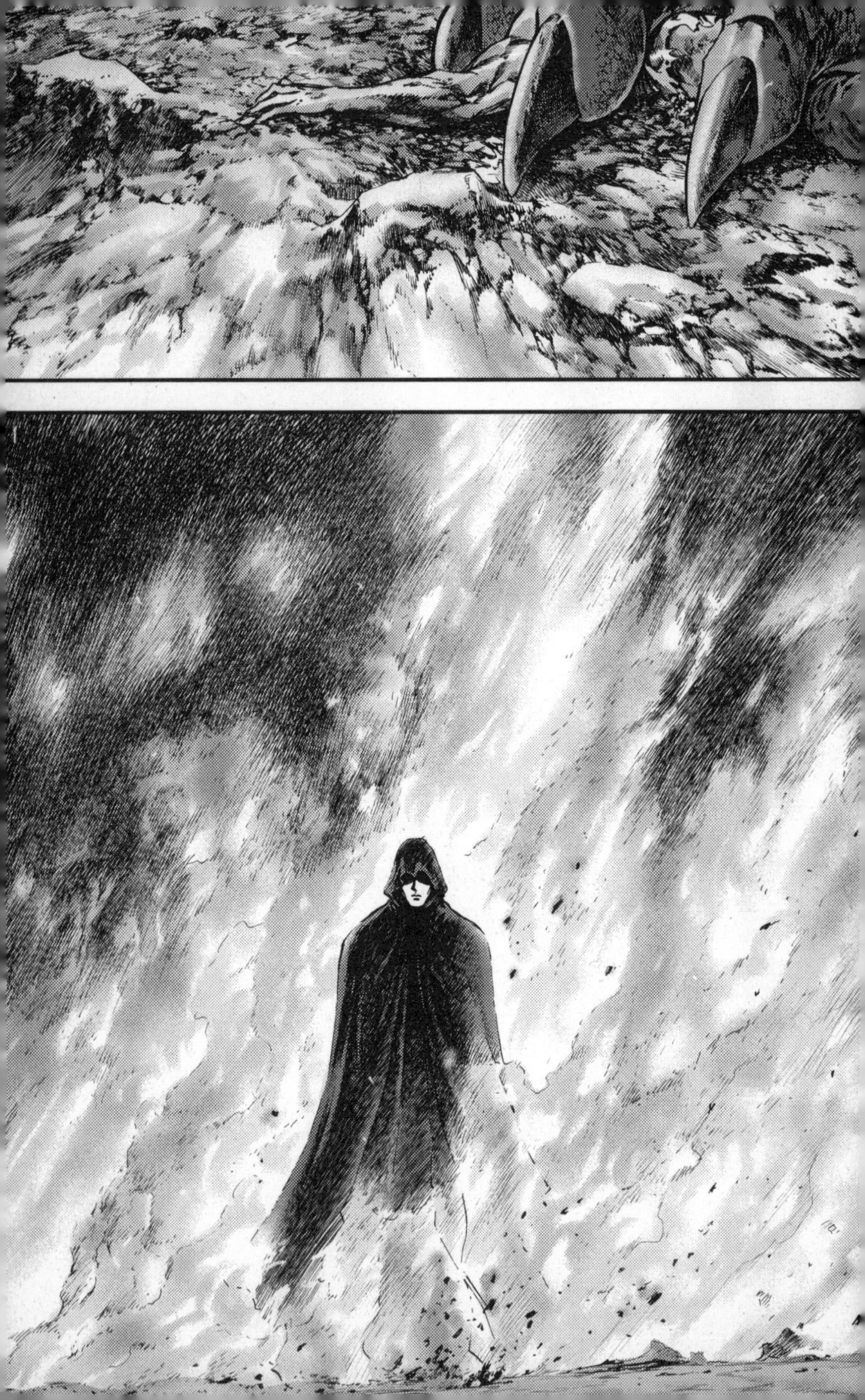

CHAPTER TWO

MASTER OF THE DEAD

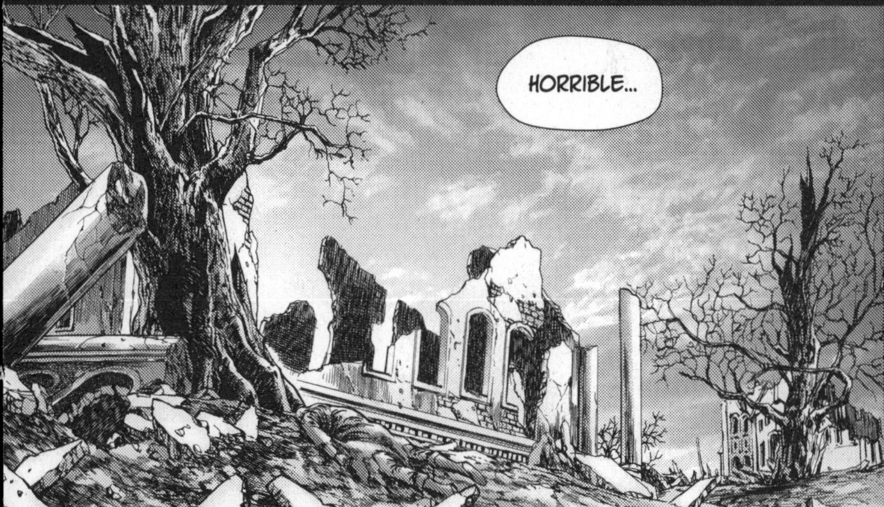
HORRIBLE...

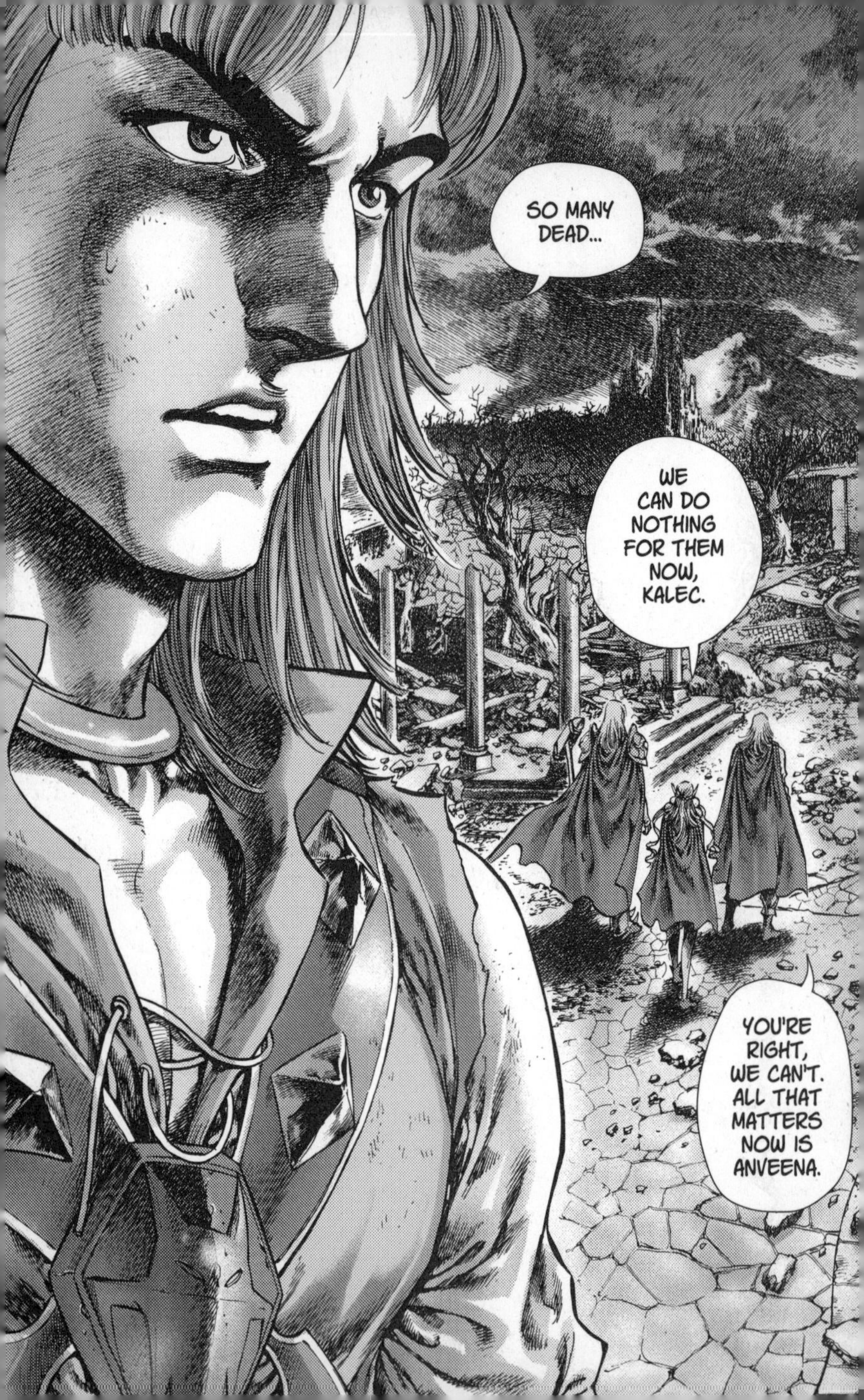
SO MANY DEAD...
WE CAN DO NOTHING FOR THEM NOW, KALEC.
YOU'RE RIGHT, WE CAN'T. ALL THAT MATTERS NOW IS ANVEENA.

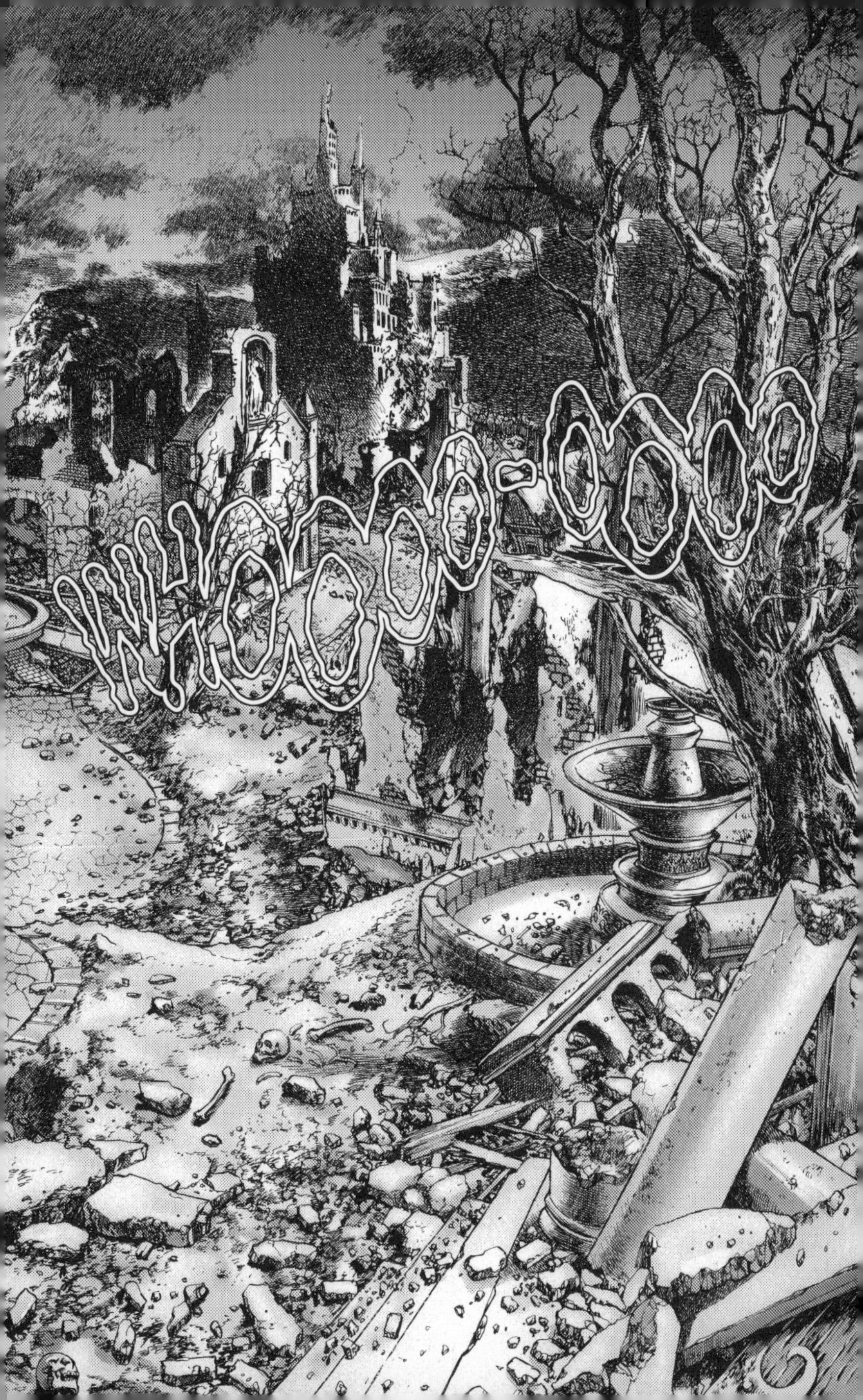
WHOOOOO-OOOO

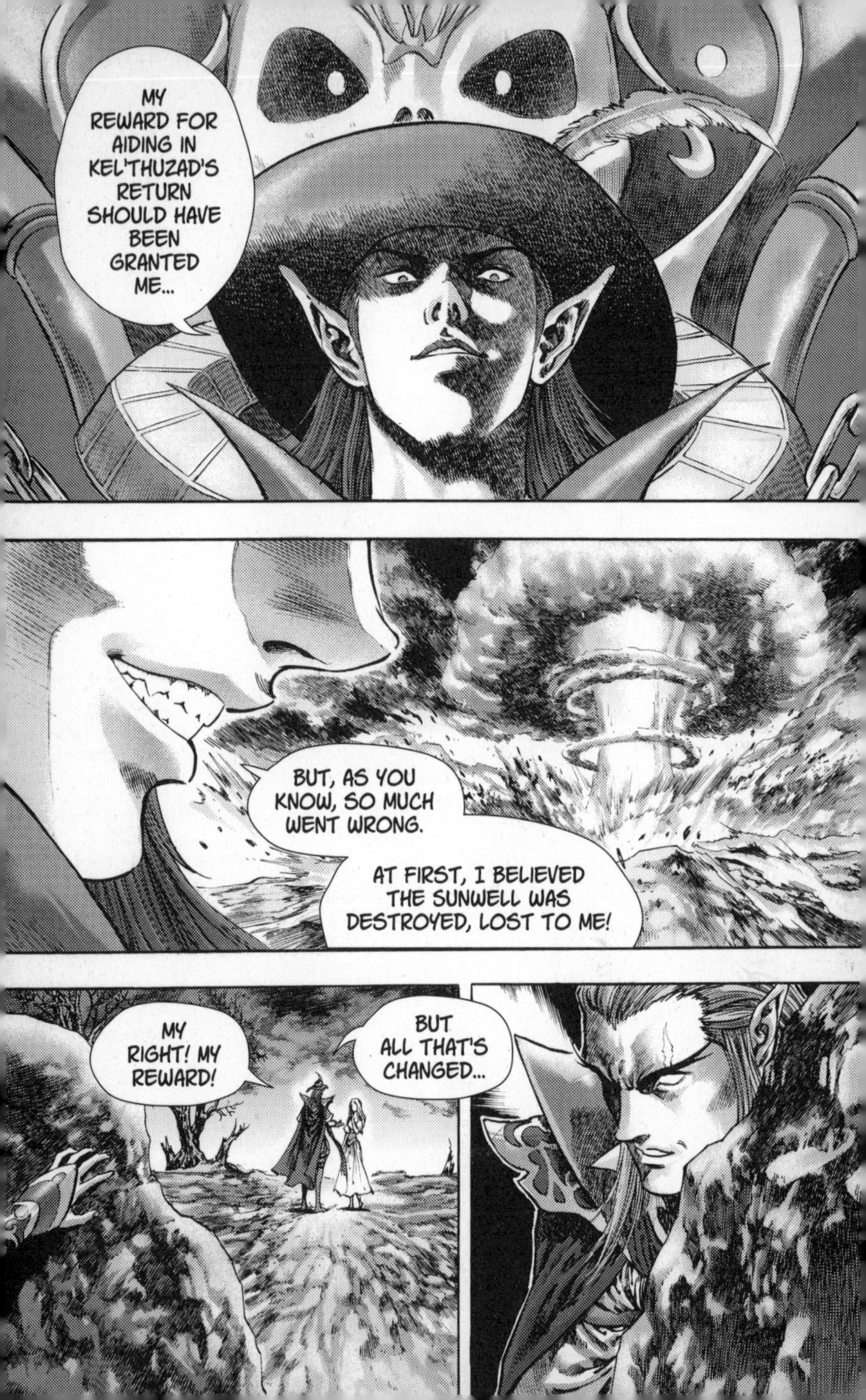
MY REWARD FOR AIDING IN KEL'THUZAD'S RETURN SHOULD HAVE BEEN GRANTED ME...
BUT, AS YOU KNOW, SO MUCH WENT WRONG.
AT FIRST, I BELIEVED THE SUNWELL WAS DESTROYED, LOST TO ME!
MY RIGHT! MY REWARD!
BUT ALL THAT'S CHANGED...

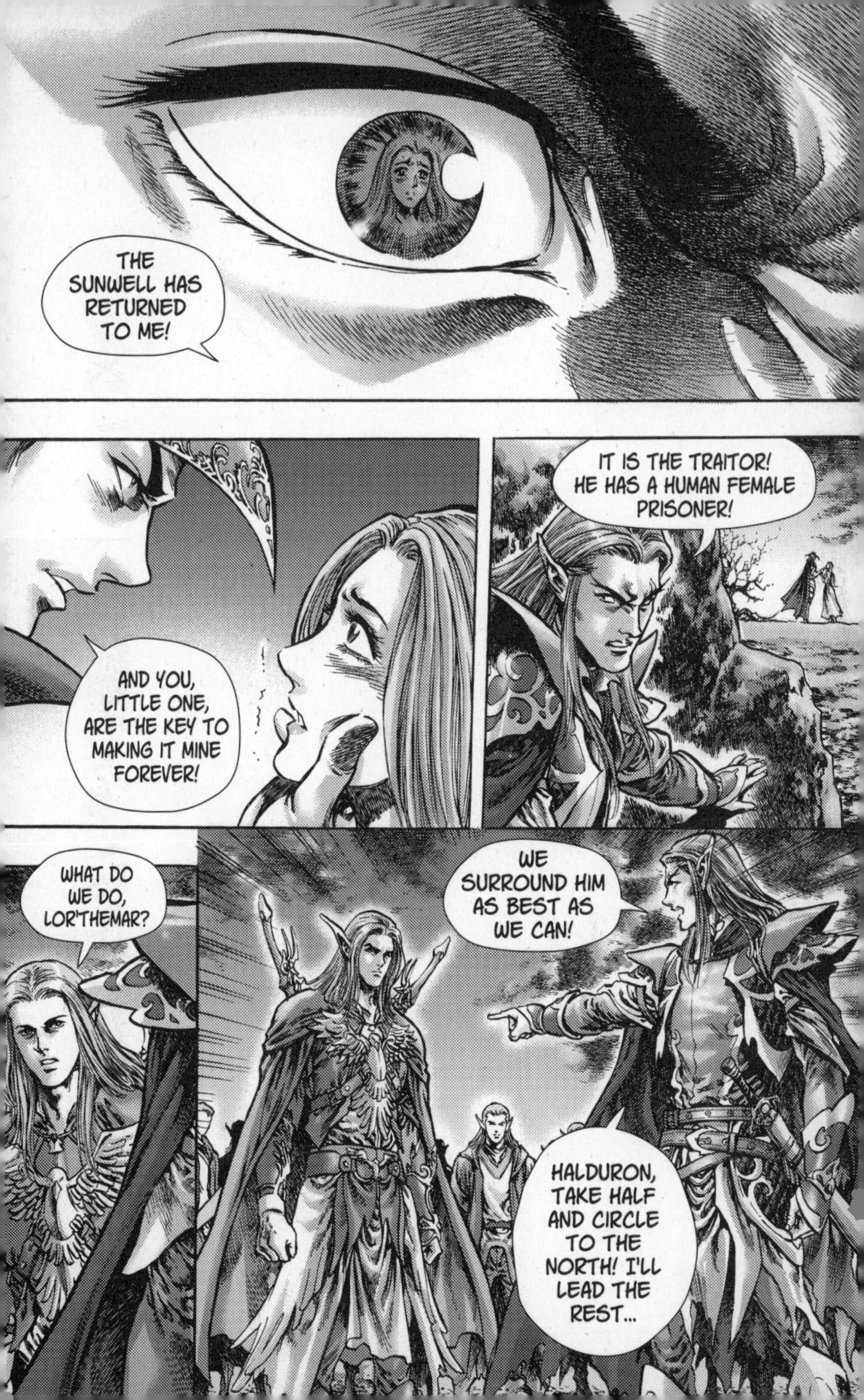
THE SUNWELL HAS RETURNED TO ME!
AND YOU, LITTLE ONE, ARE THE KEY TO MAKING IT MINE FOREVER!
IT IS THE TRAITOR! HE HAS A HUMAN FEMALE PRISONER!
WHAT DO WE DO, LOR'THEMAR?
WE SURROUND HIM AS BEST AS WE CAN!
HALDURON, TAKE HALF AND CIRCLE TO THE NORTH! I'LL LEAD THE REST...

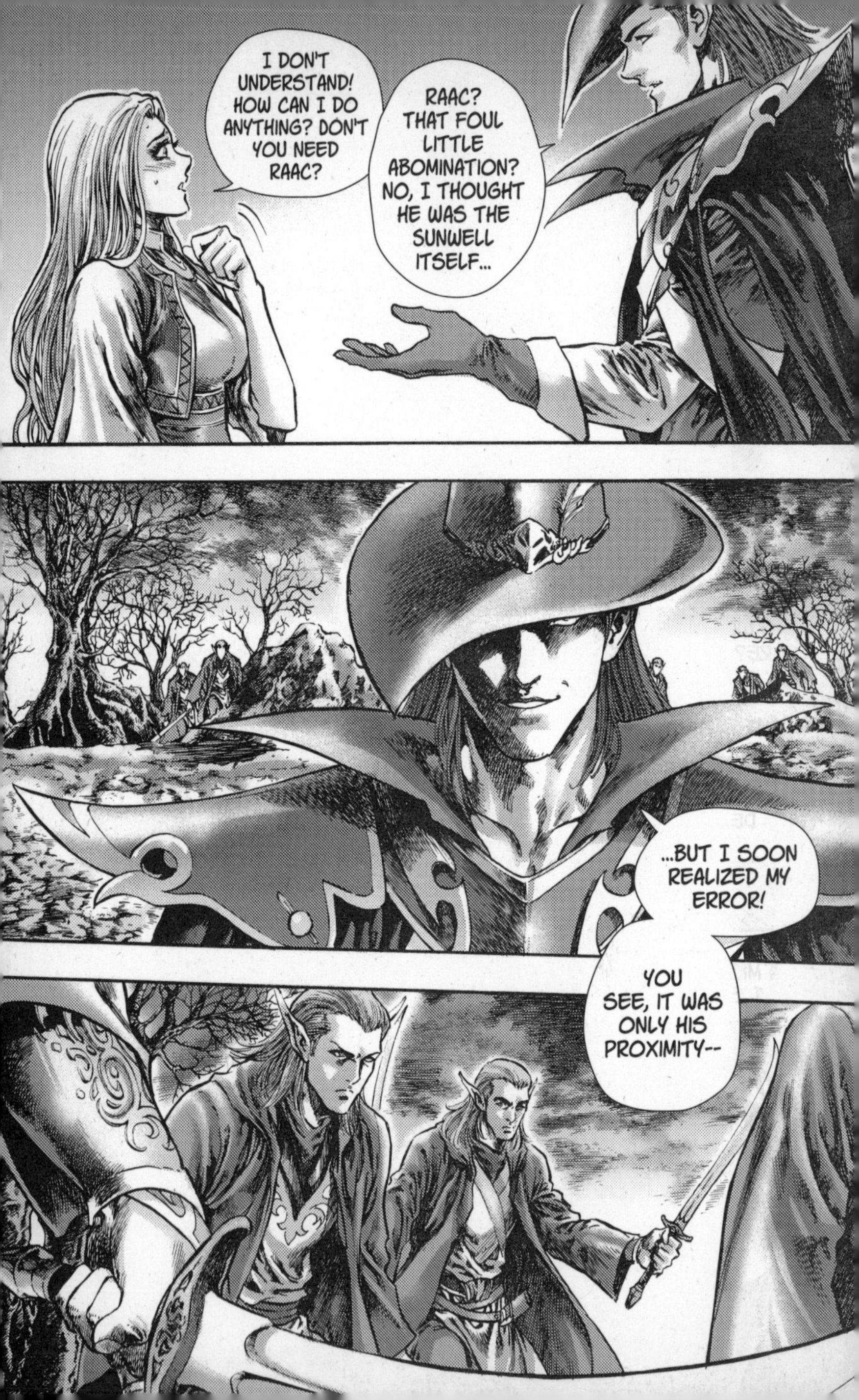
I DON'T UNDERSTAND! HOW CAN I DO ANYTHING? DON'T YOU NEED RAAC?
RAAC? THAT FOUL LITTLE ABOMINATION? NO, I THOUGHT HE WAS THE SUNWELL ITSELF...
...BUT I SOON REALIZED MY ERROR!
YOU SEE, IT WAS ONLY HIS PROXIMITY--

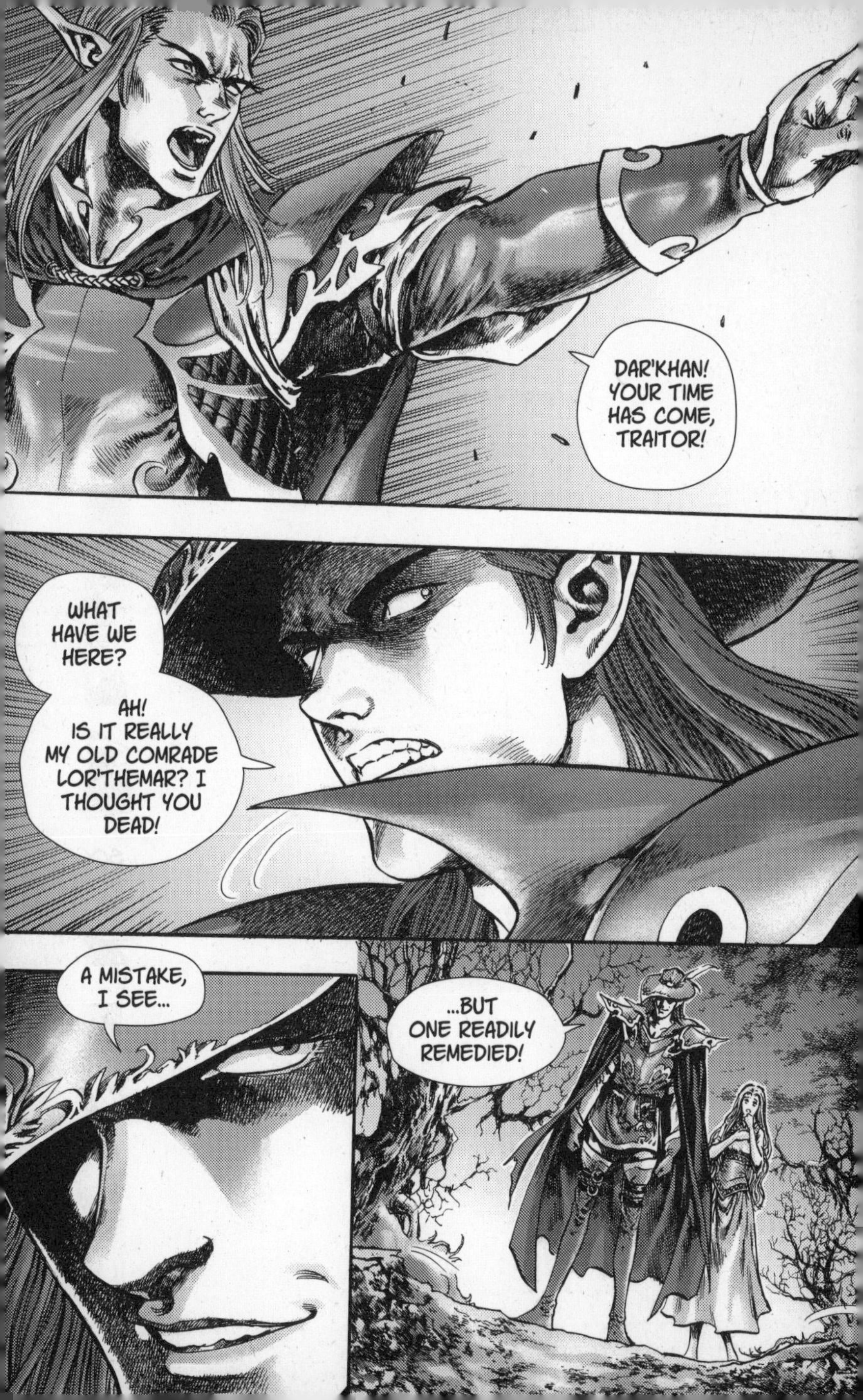
DAR'KHAN! YOUR TIME HAS COME, TRAITOR!
WHAT HAVE WE HERE?
AH! IS IT REALLY MY OLD COMRADE LOR'THEMAR? I THOUGHT YOU DEAD!
A MISTAKE, I SEE...
...BUT ONE READILY REMEDIED!

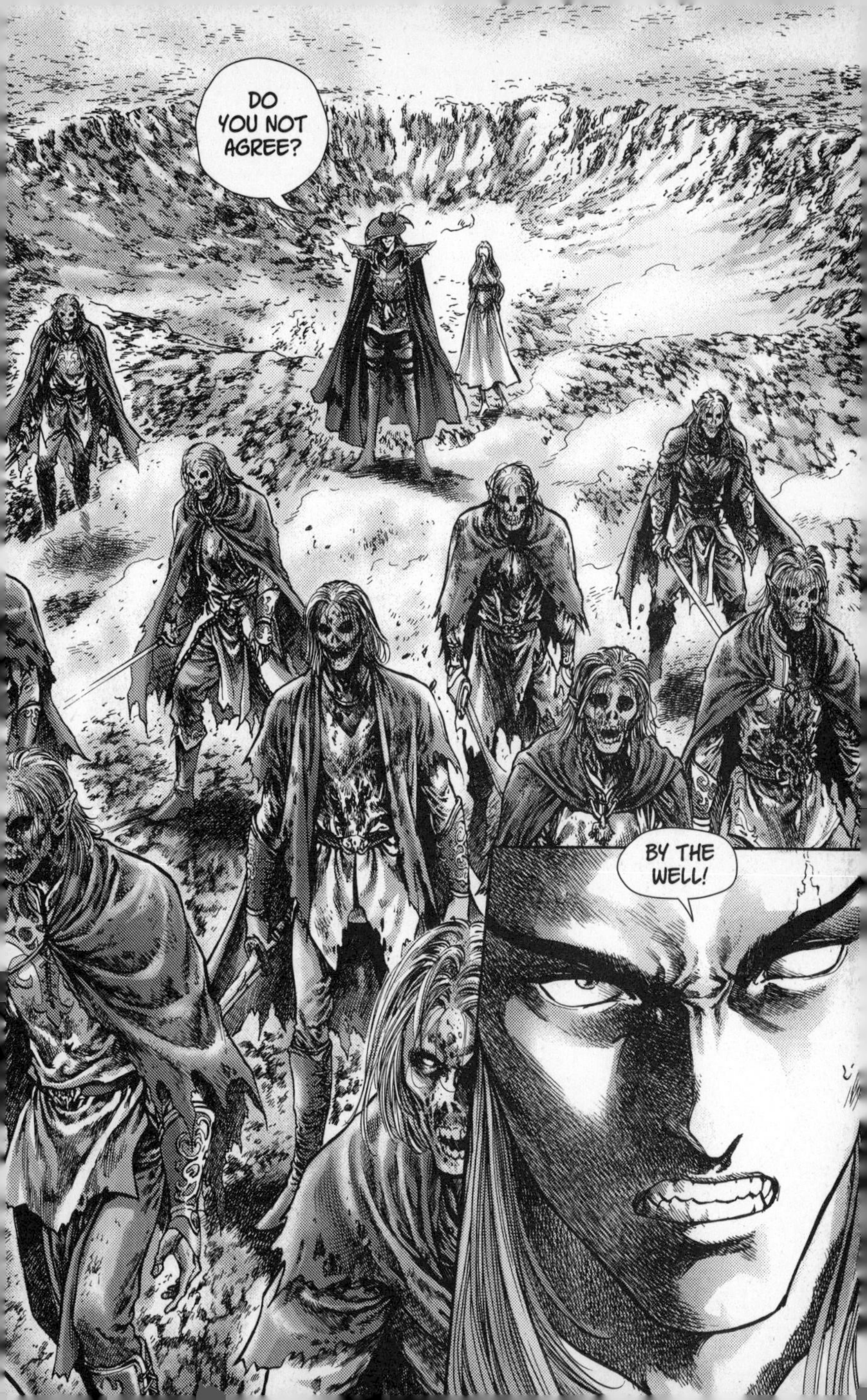
DO YOU NOT AGREE?
BY THE WELL!

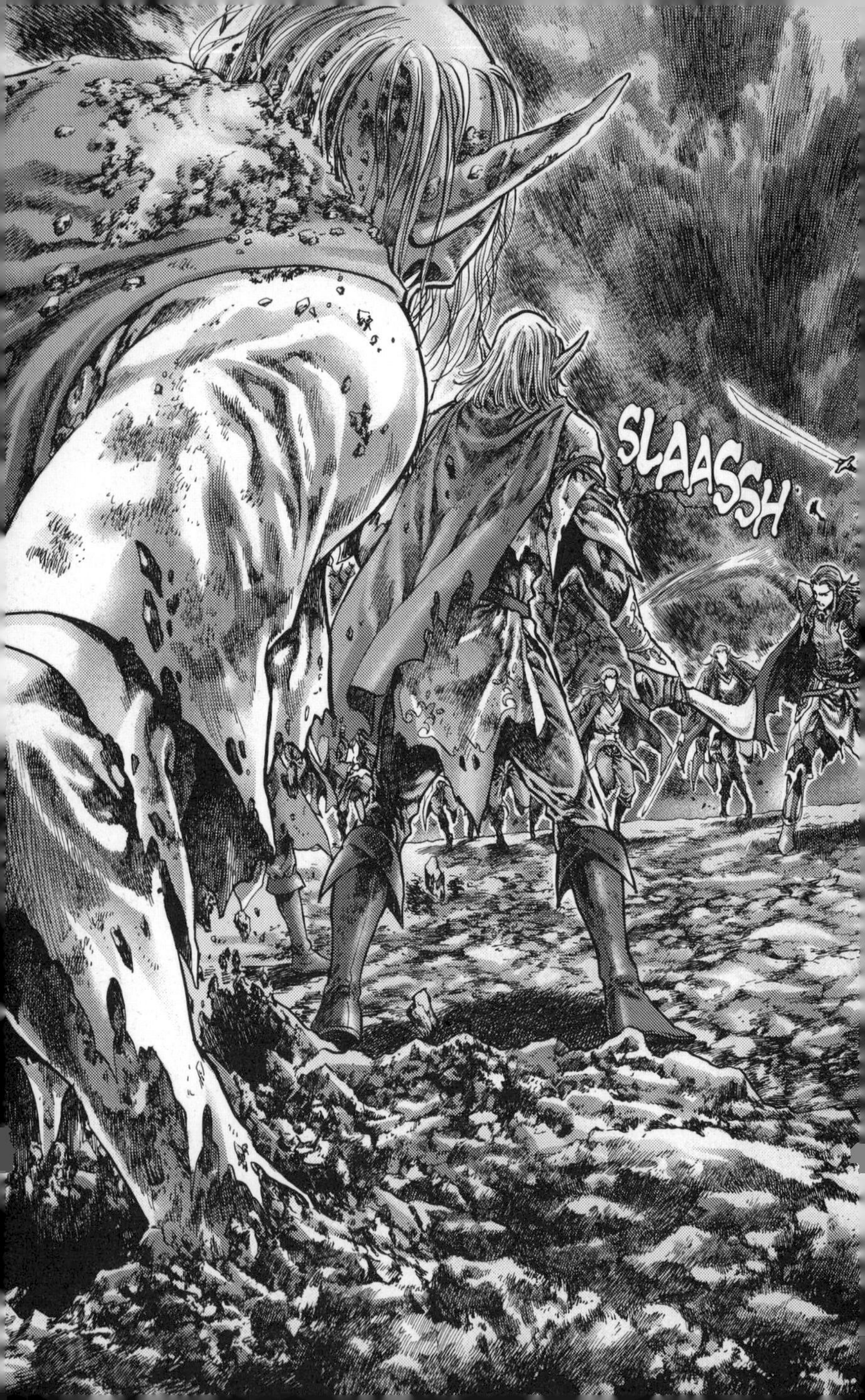
SLAASSH

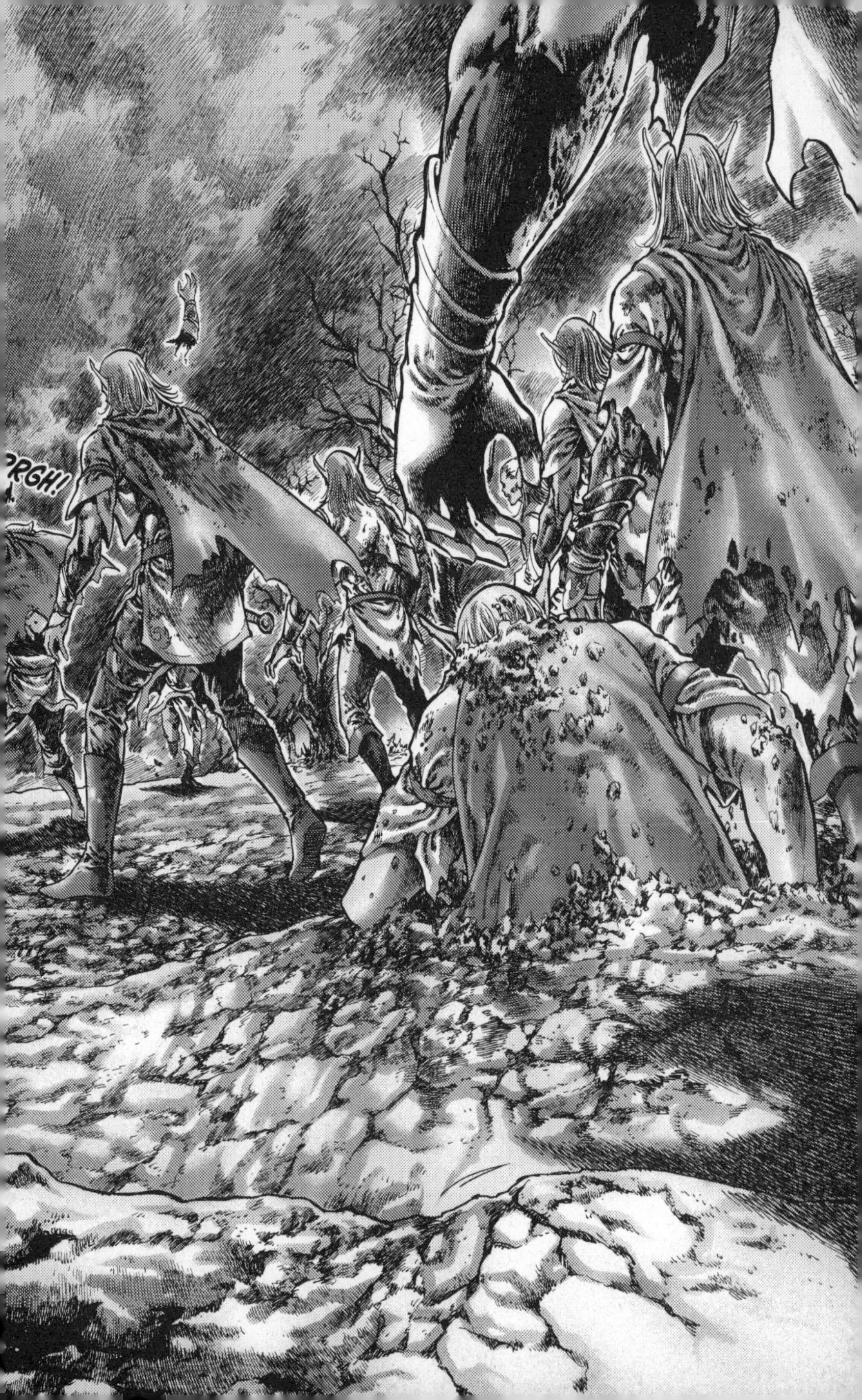
RGH!

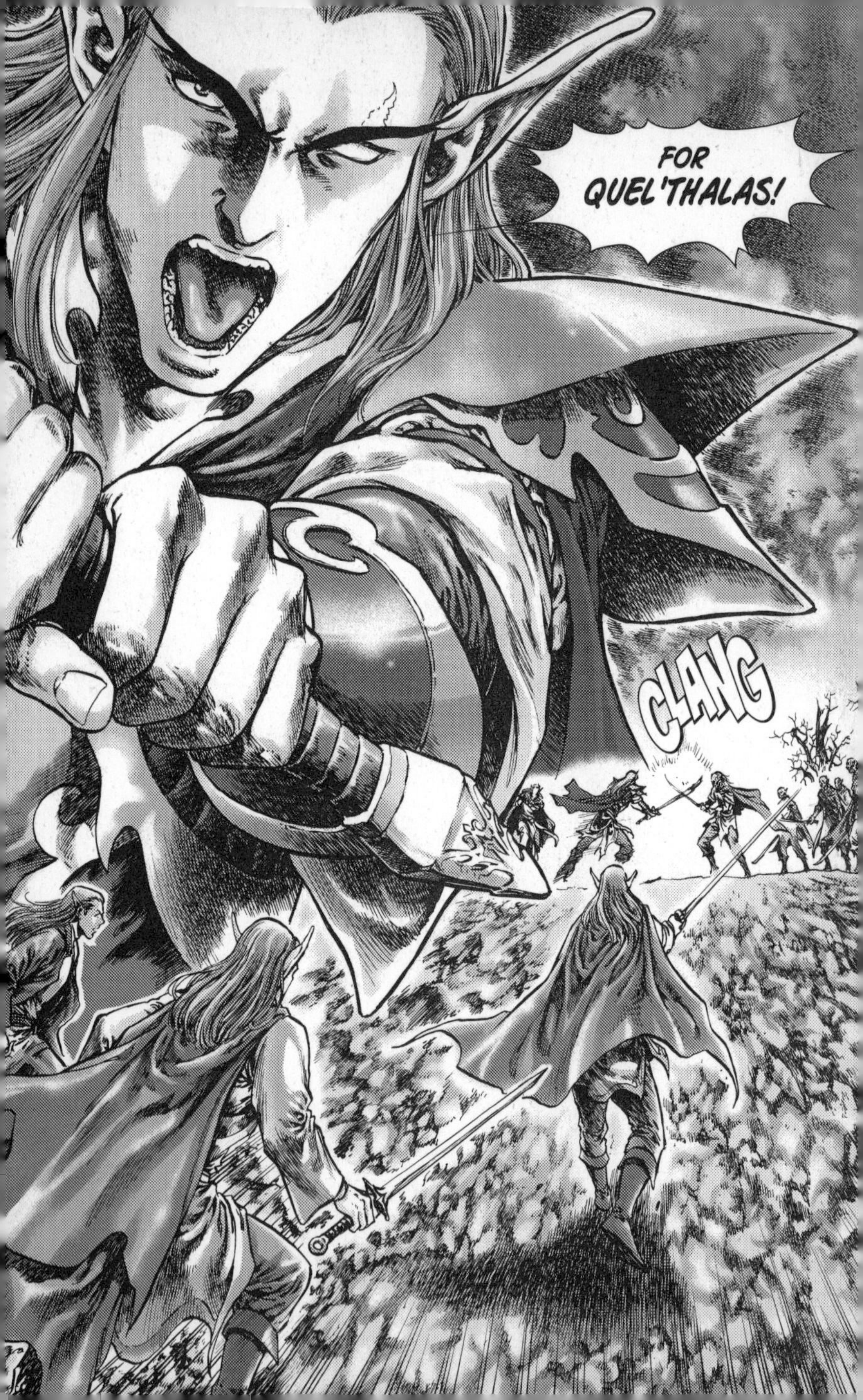
FOR QUEL'THALAS!
CLANG

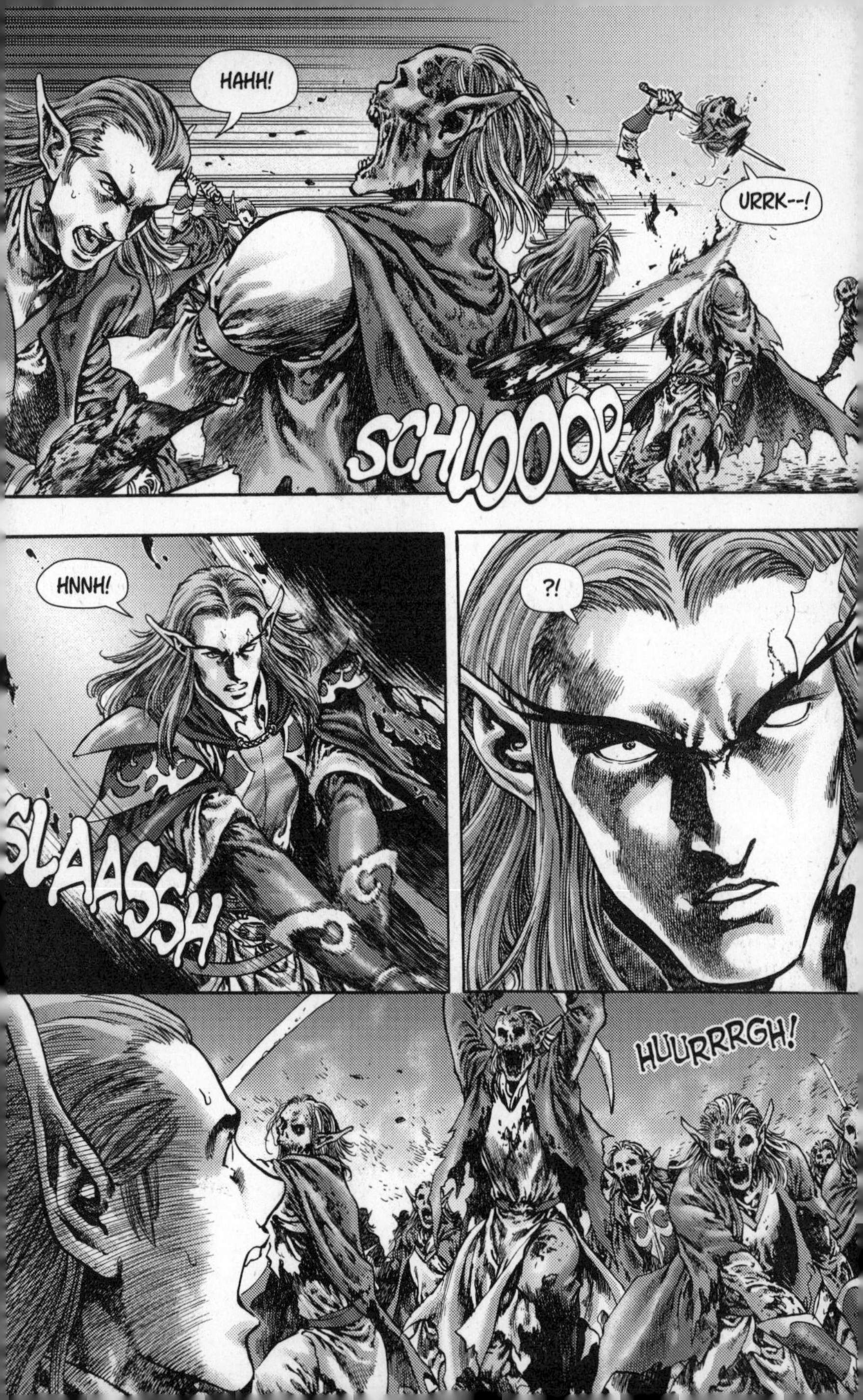
HAHH!
URRK--!
SCHLOOOP
HNNH!
SLAASSH
?!
HUURRRGH!

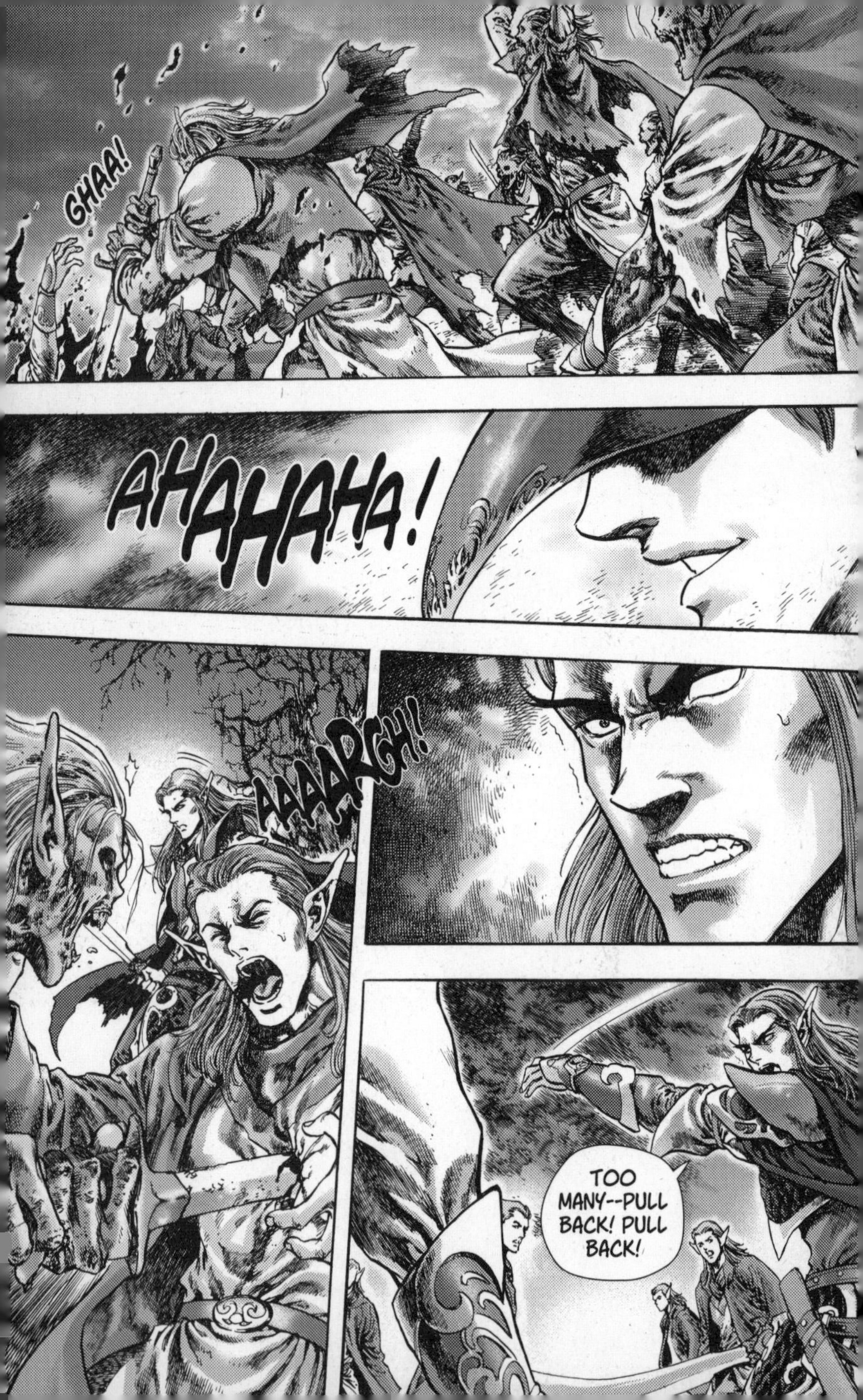
GHAA!
AHAHAHA!
AAAARGH!
TOO MANY--PULL BACK! PULL BACK!

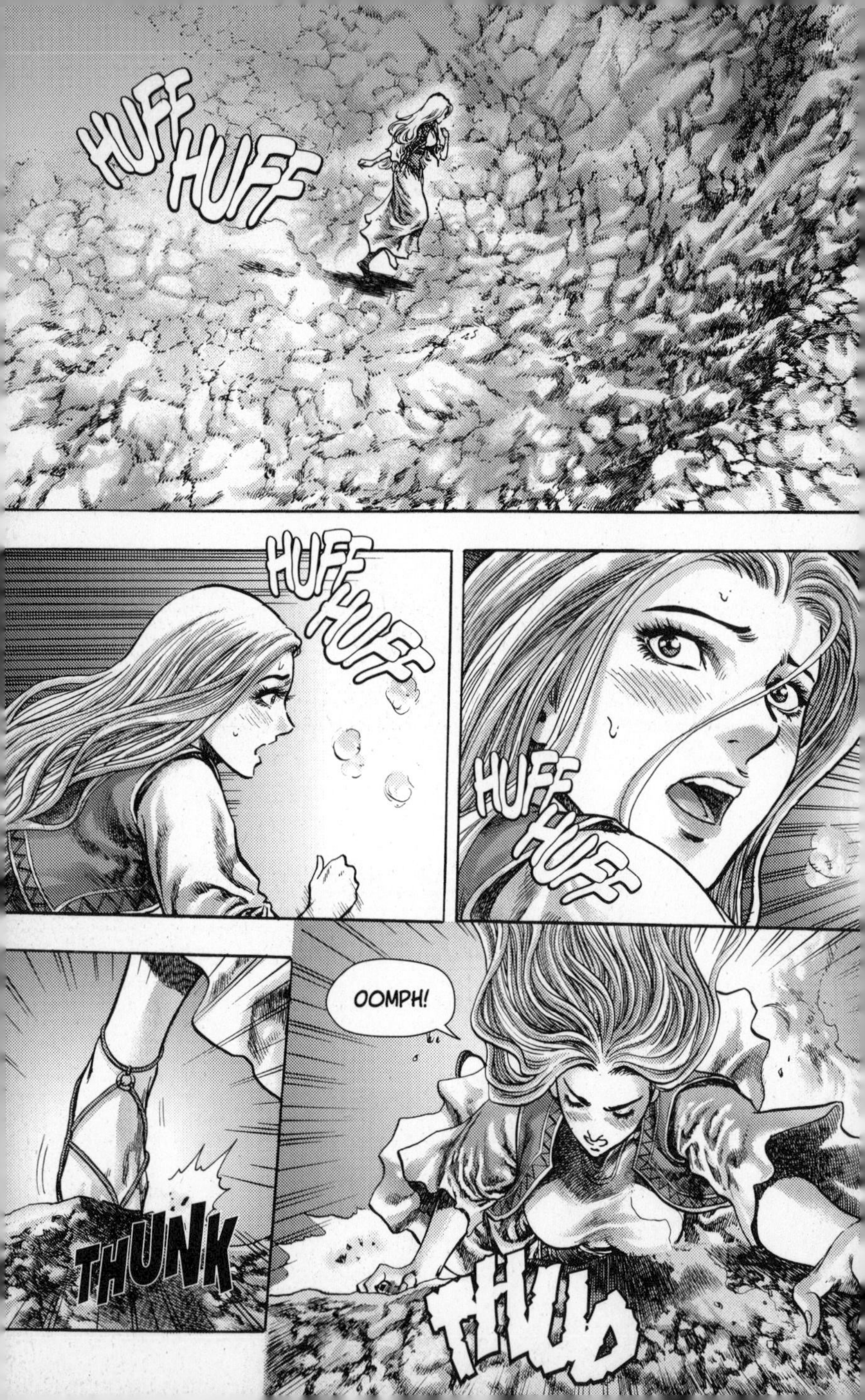
HUFF HUFF
HUFF HUFF
HUFF HUFF
THUNK
OOMPH!
THUD

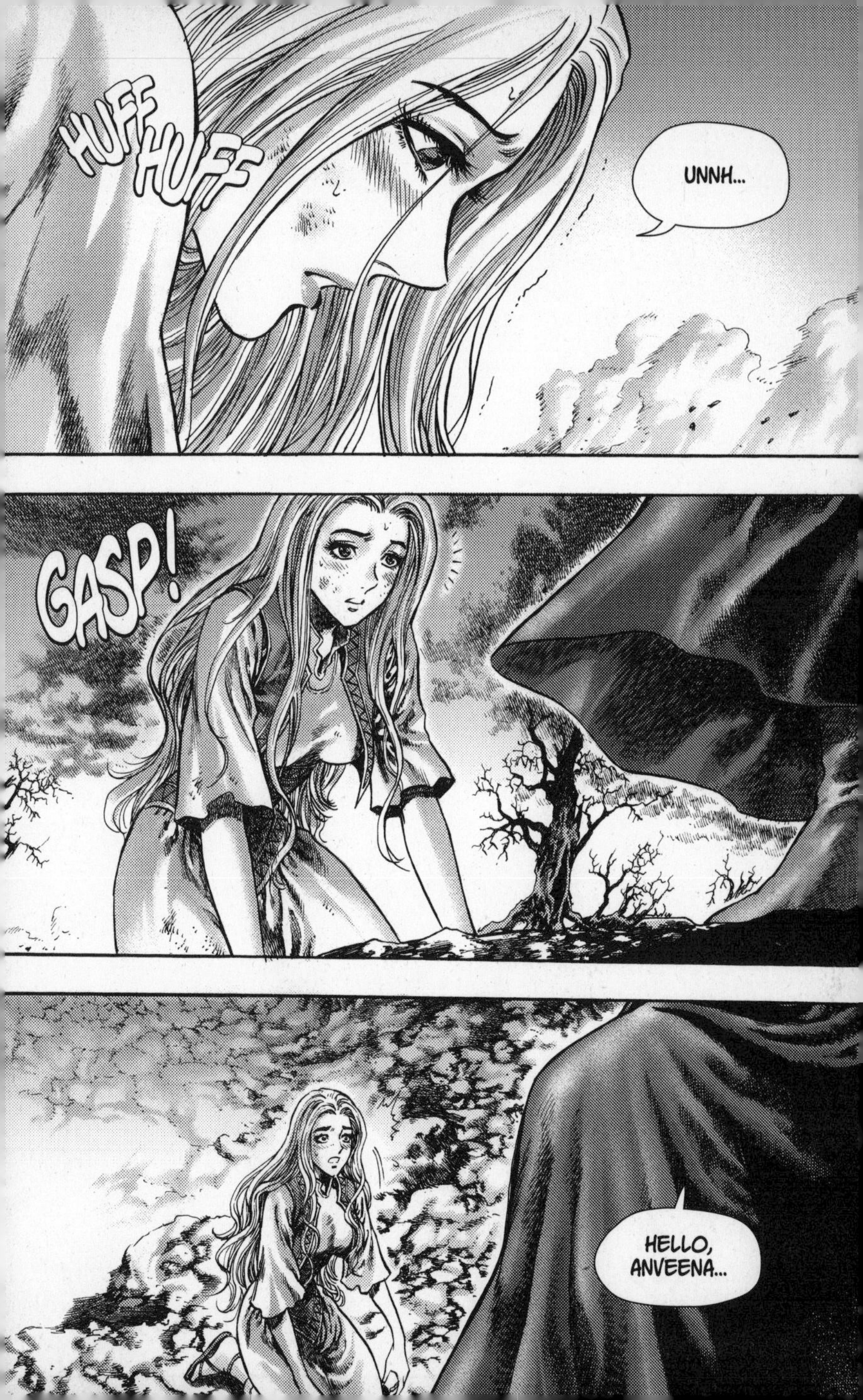
HUFF HUFF
UNNH...
GASP!
HELLO, ANVEENA...

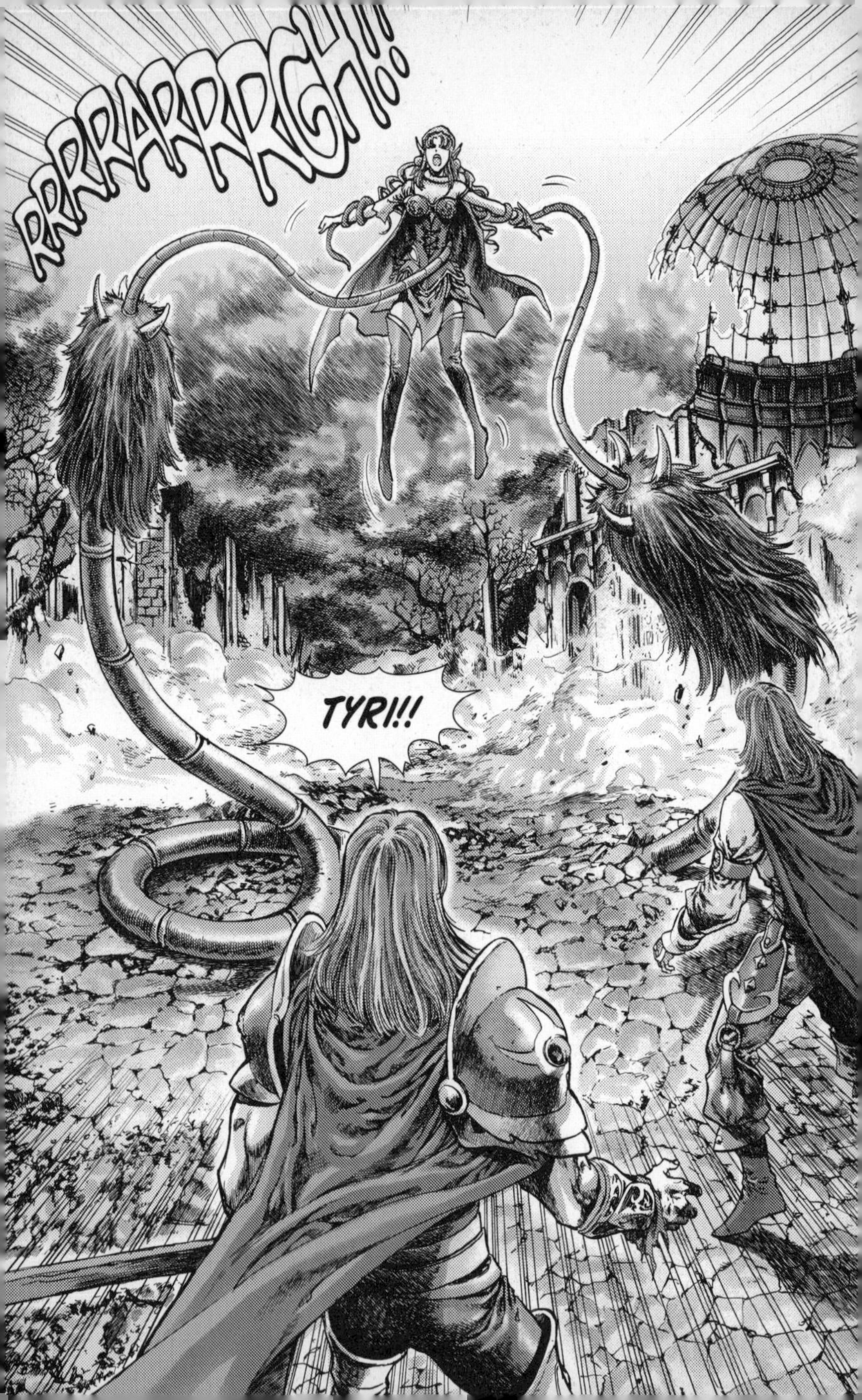
RRRRAARRRGH!!
TYRI!!

CHAPTER THREE

CRY OF THE BANSHEE

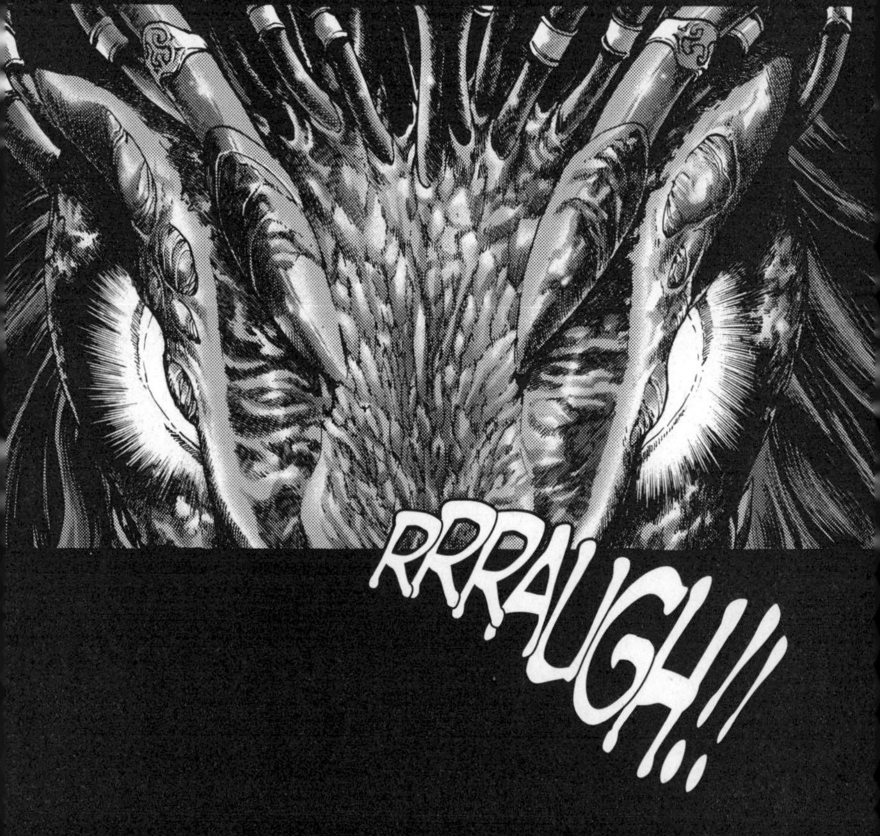
RRRRAUGH!!

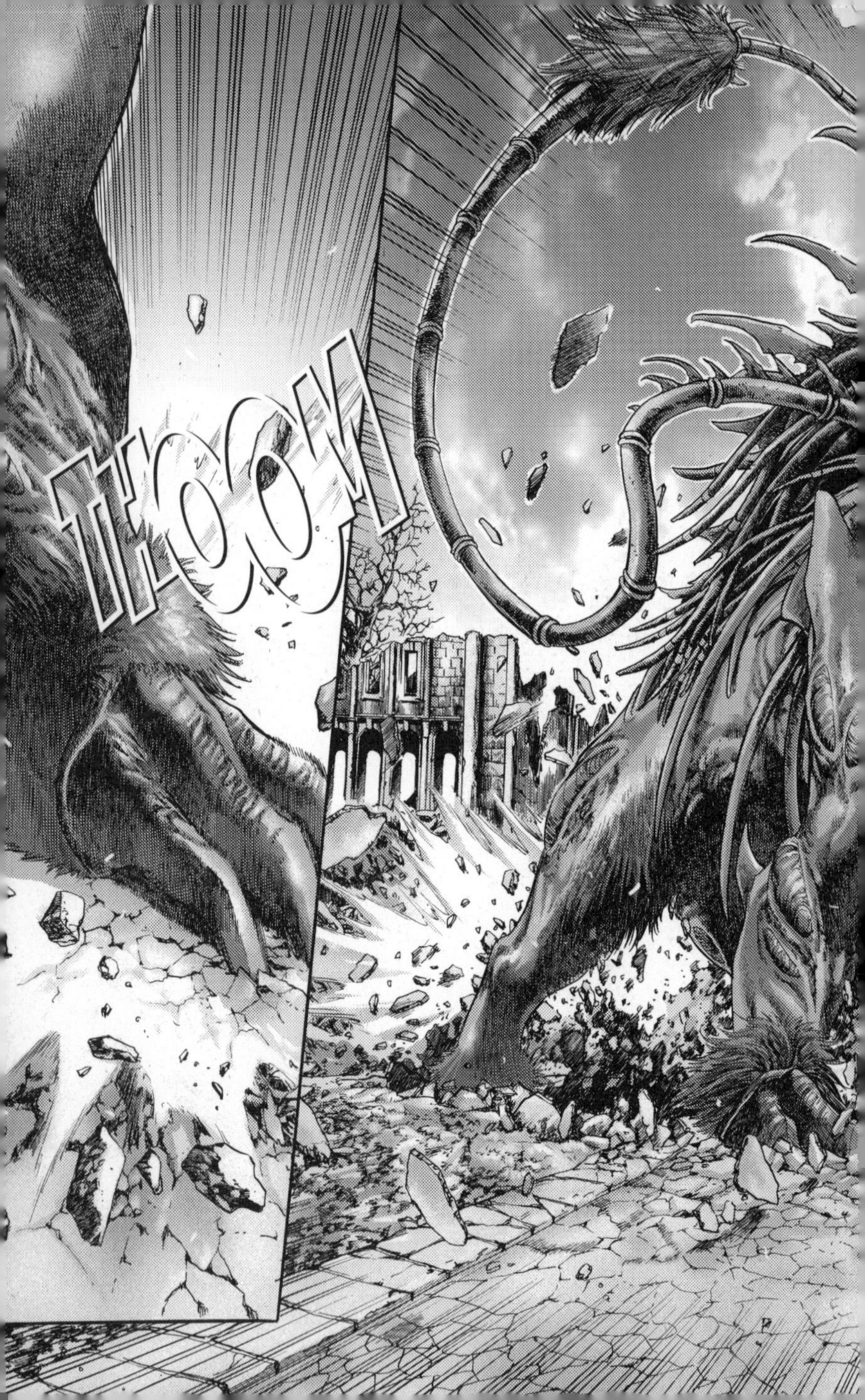
THOOM

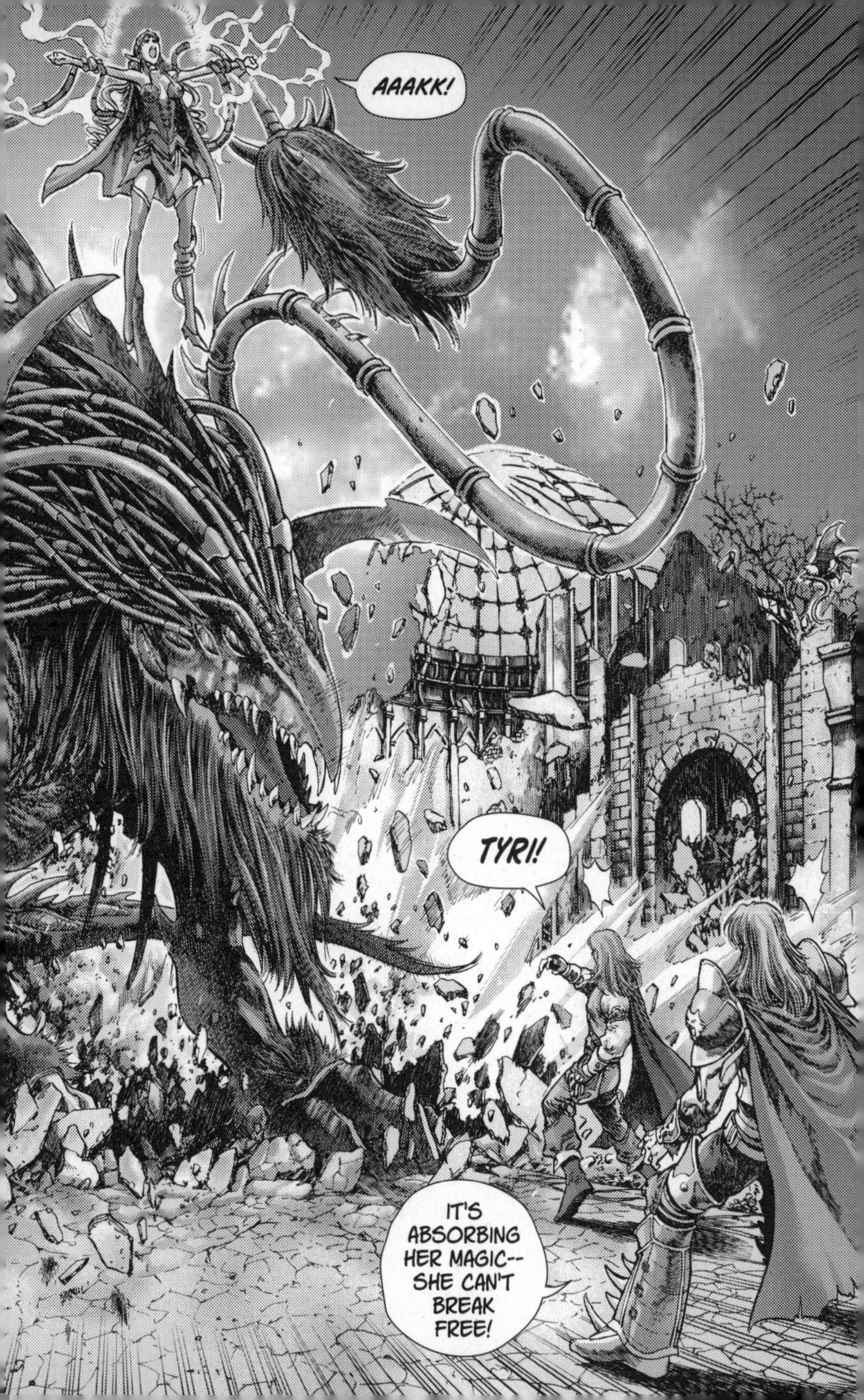
AAAKK!
TYRI!
IT'S ABSORBING HER MAGIC-- SHE CAN'T BREAK FREE!

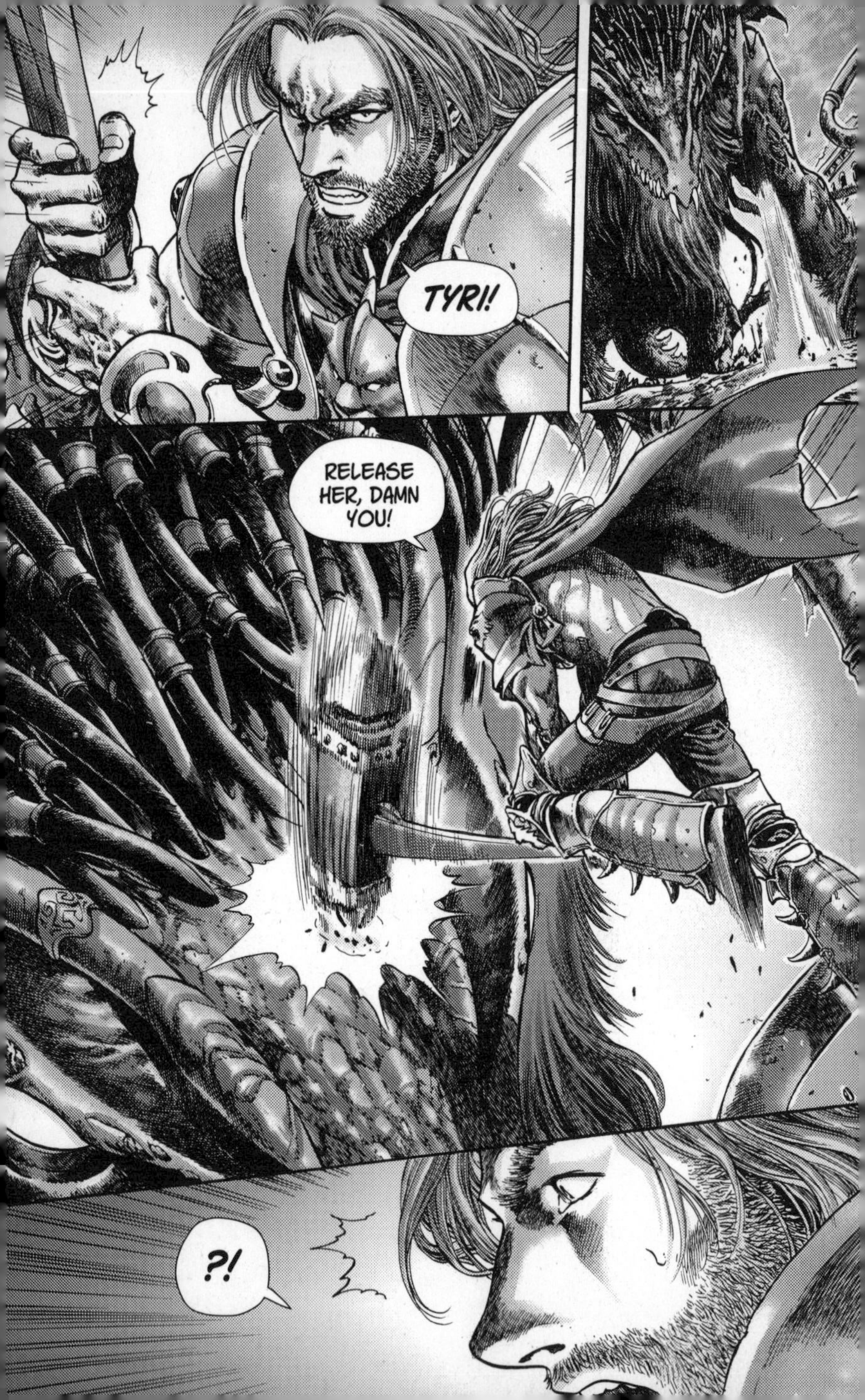
TYRI!
RELEASE HER, DAMN YOU!
?!

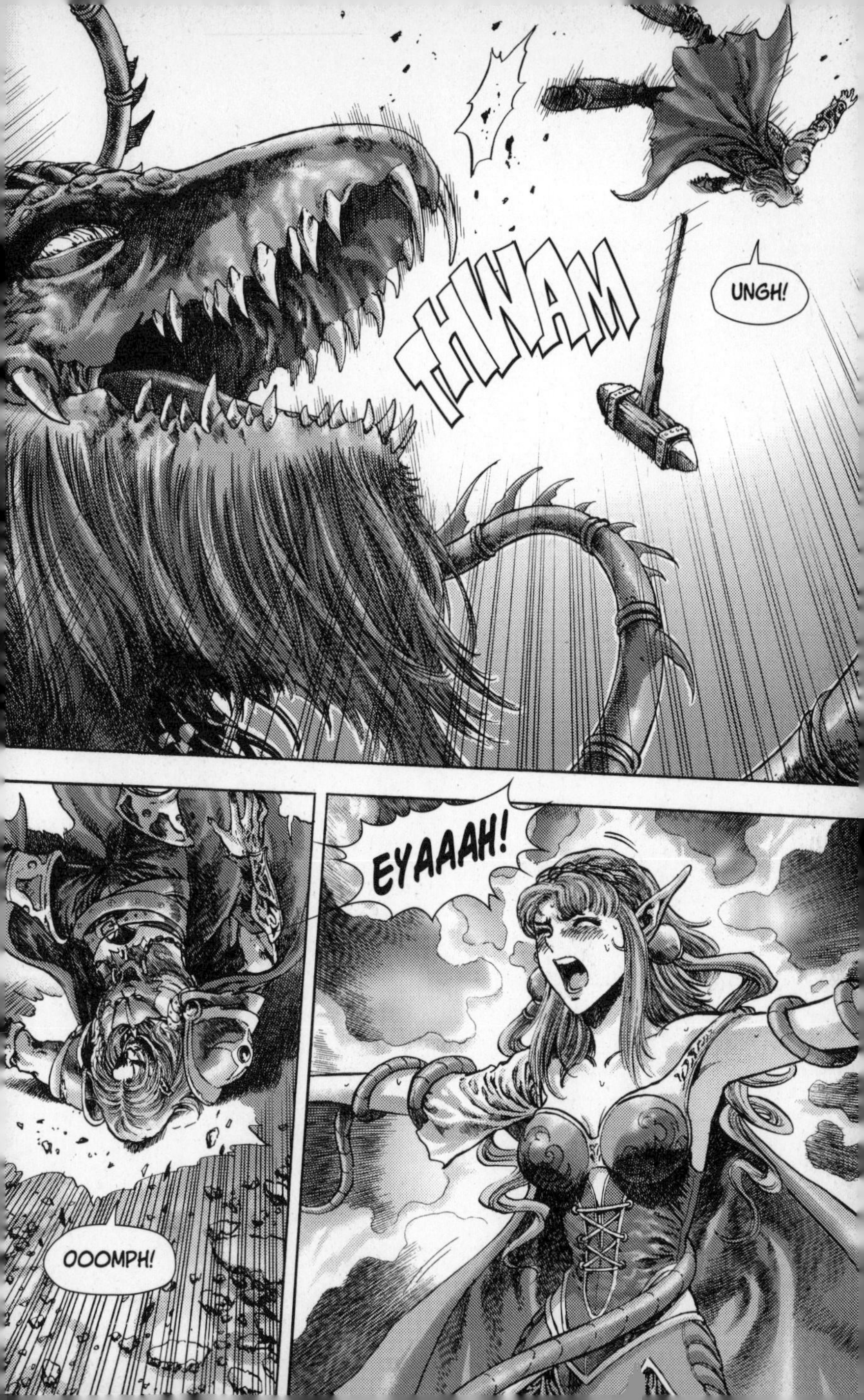
THWAM
UNGH!
OOOMPH!
EYAAAH!

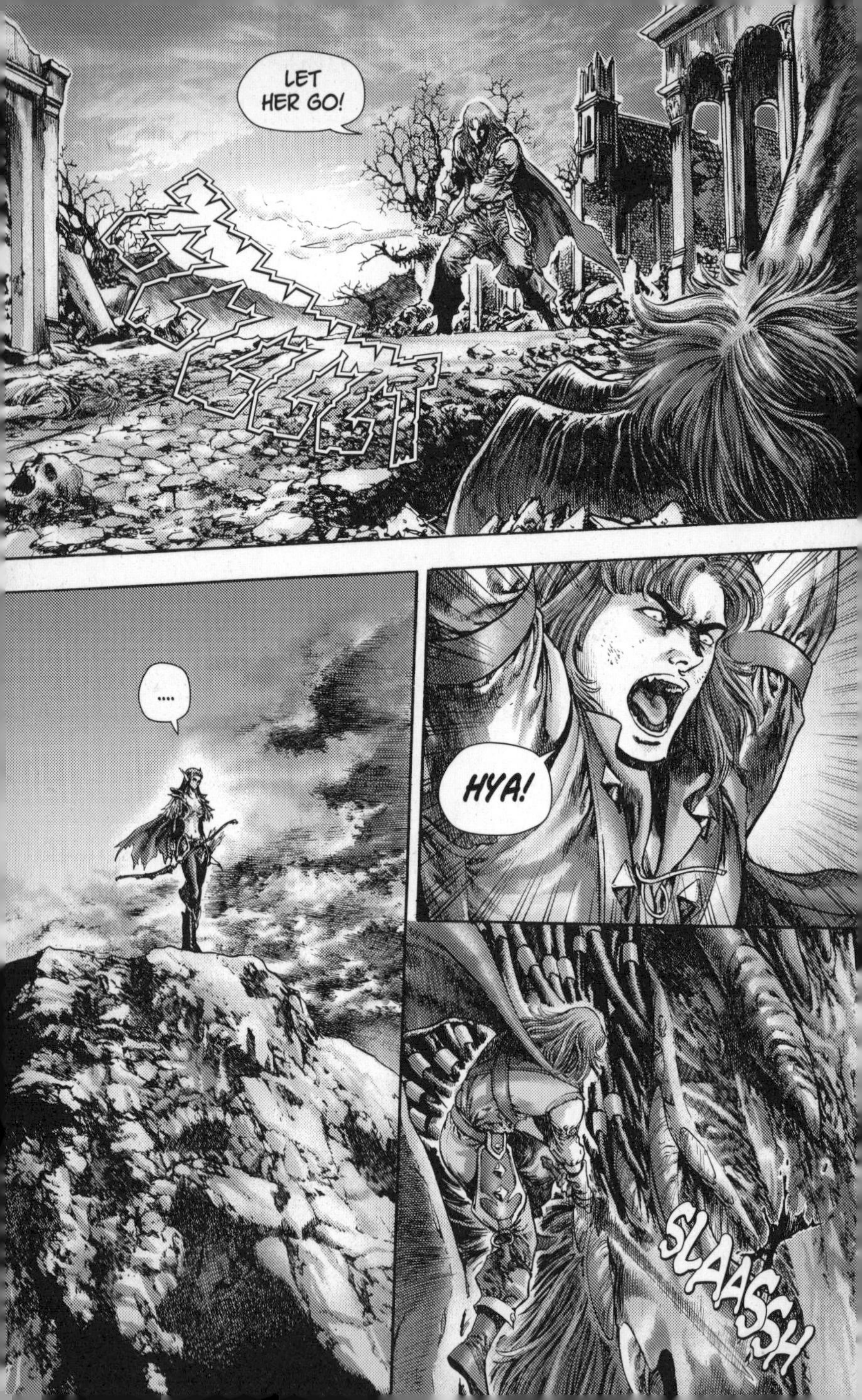
LET HER GO!
....
HYA!
SLAASSH

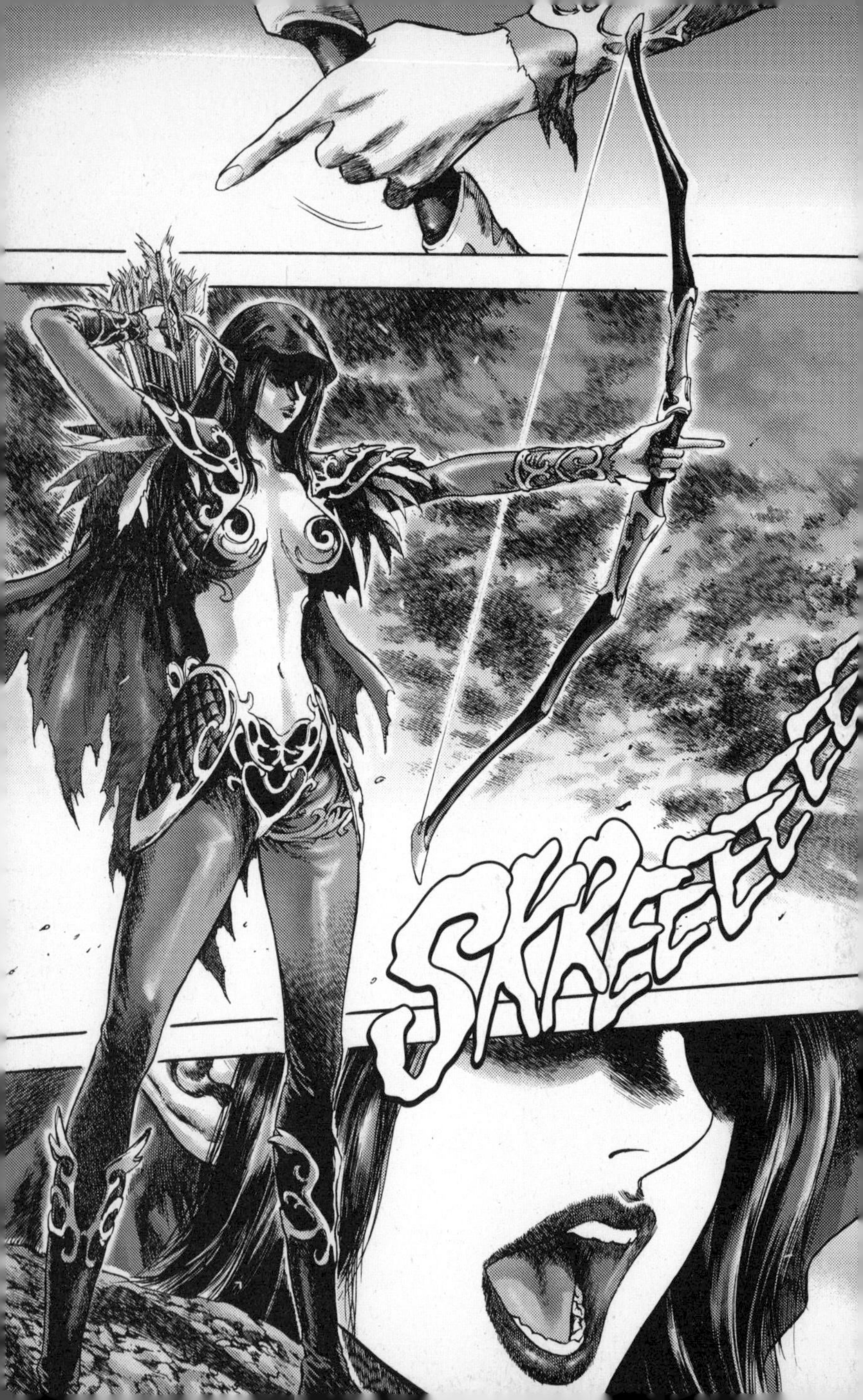
SKREEEEEEE

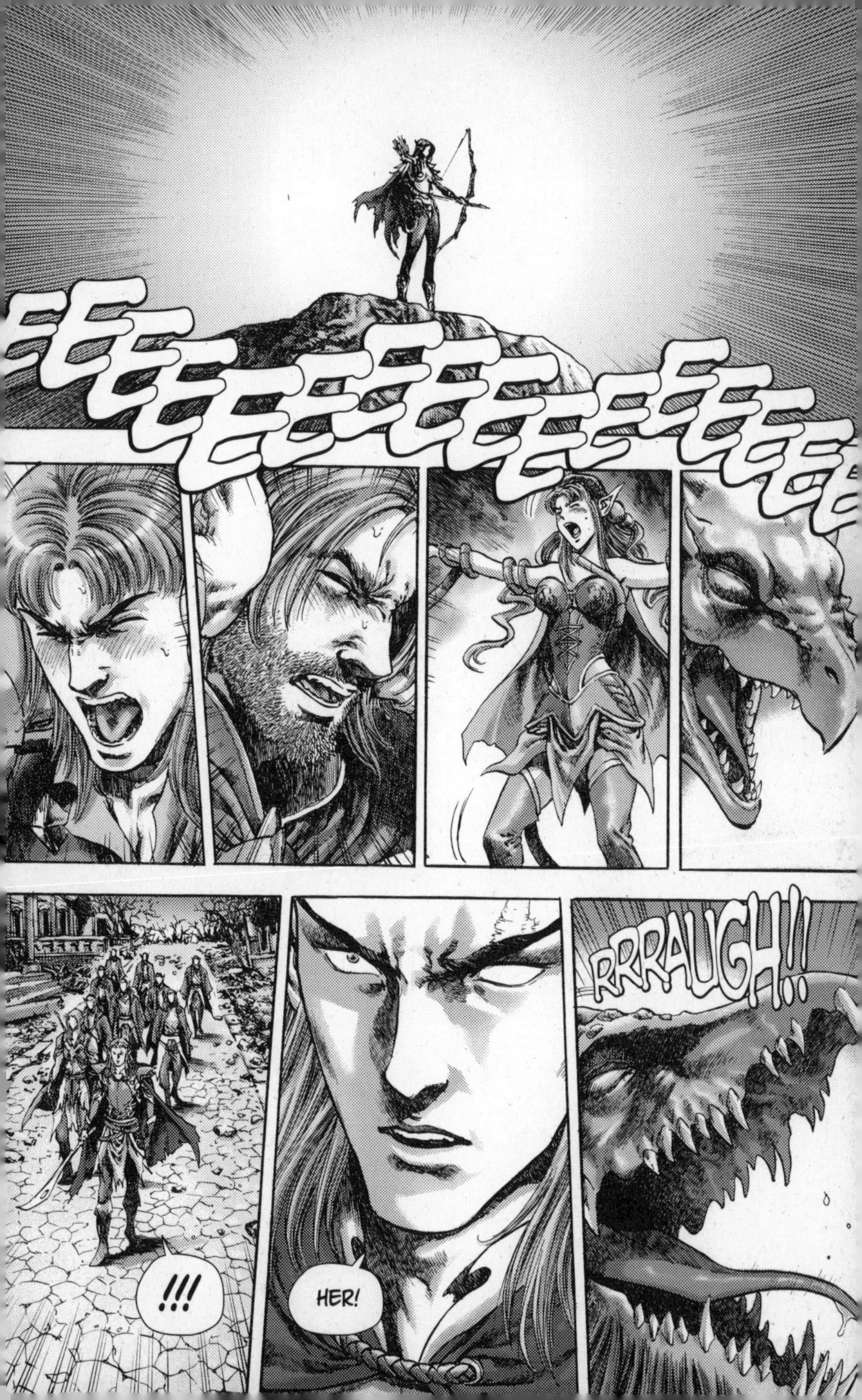
EEEEEEEEEEEEEEEEEEEEEEEEEEEEEEE
!!!
HER!
RRRAUGH!!

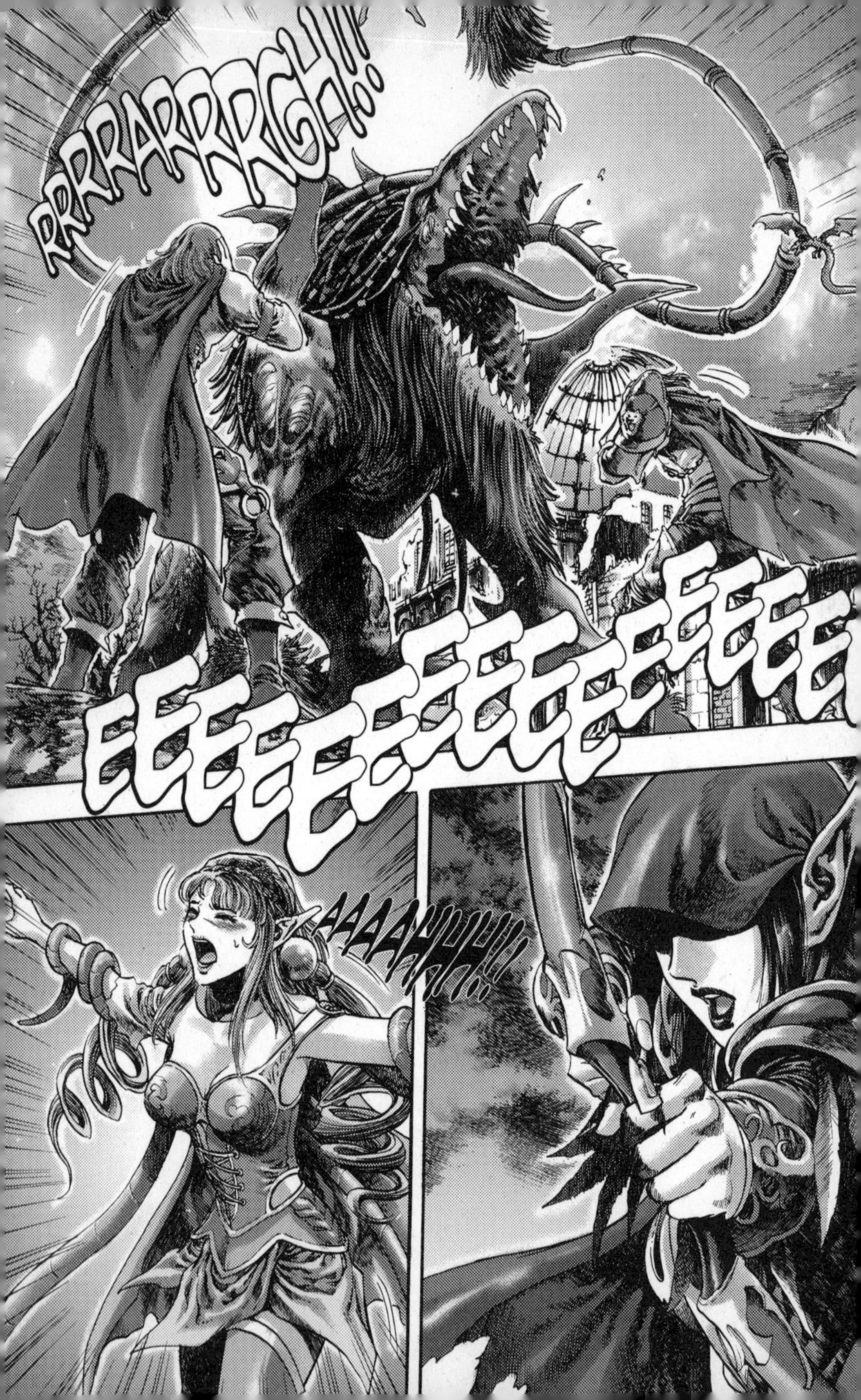
RRRRARRRGH!!!
EEEEEEEEEEEEEEEEEEE
AAAAAHHHH!!!

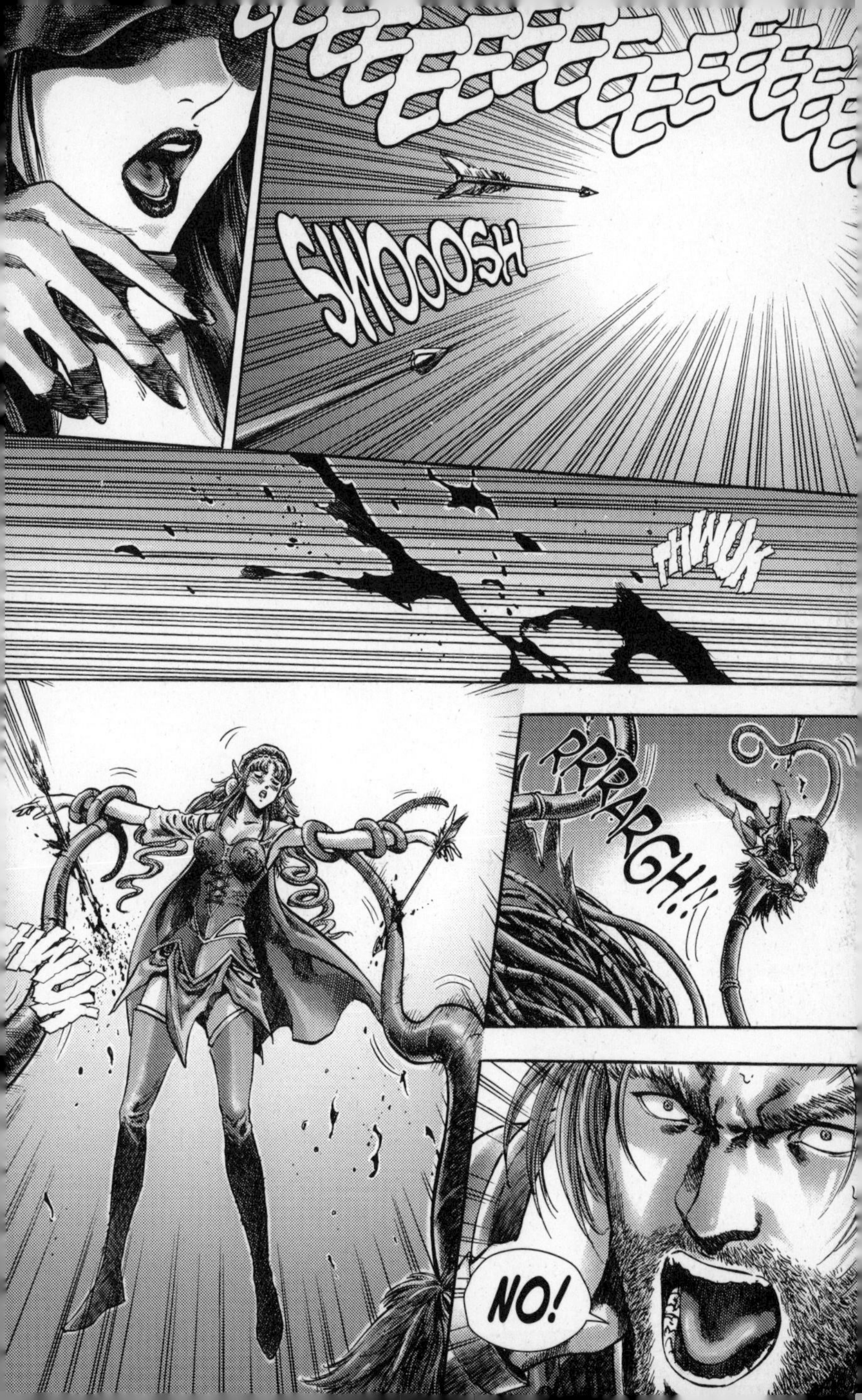
EEEEEEEEEEEEEEEEEEEEE
SWOOOSH
THWUK
THWUK
RRRARGH!!!
NO!

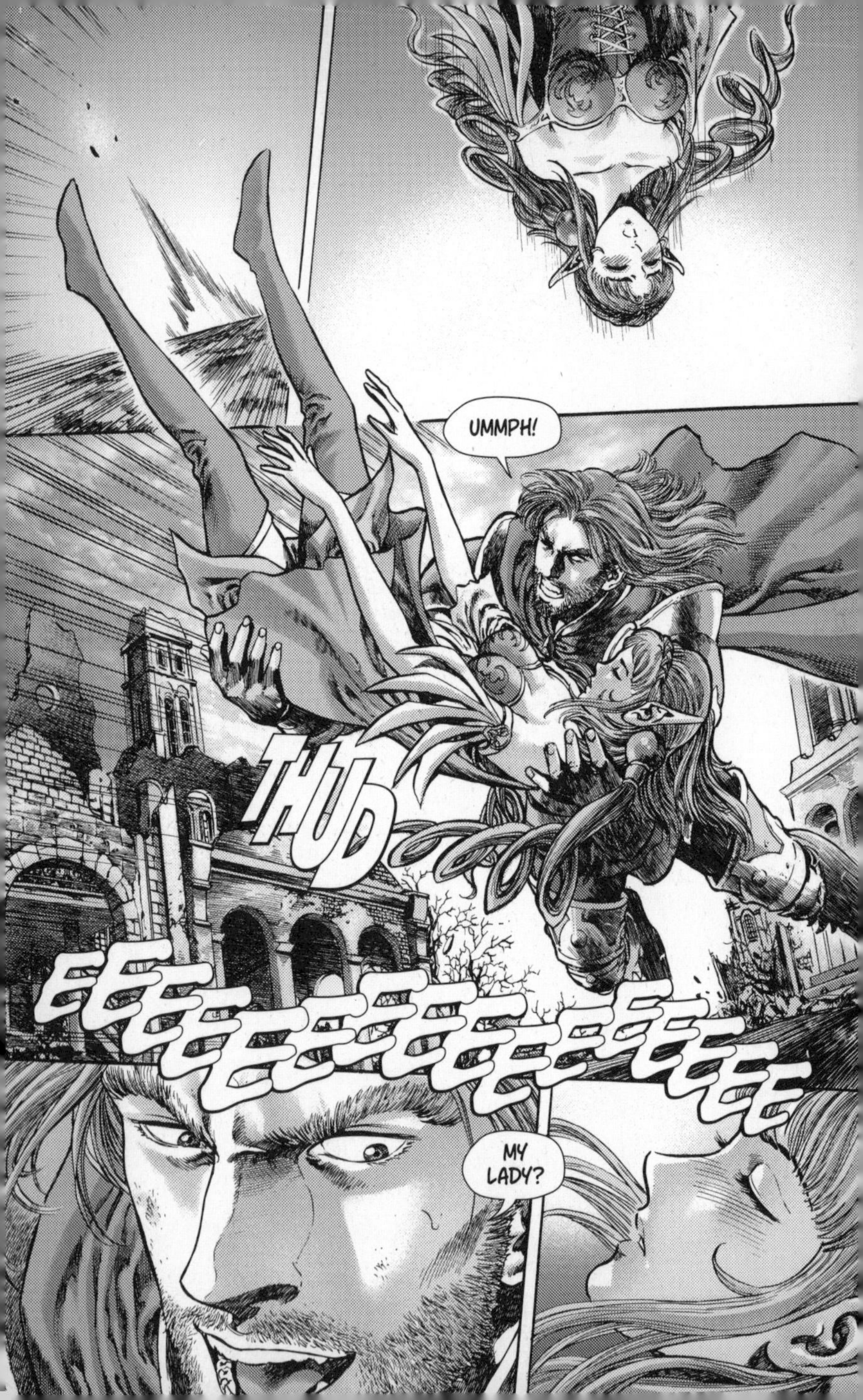
UMMPH!
THUD
EEEEEEEEEEEEEEEEEEEEEEEEEEEEEE
MY LADY?

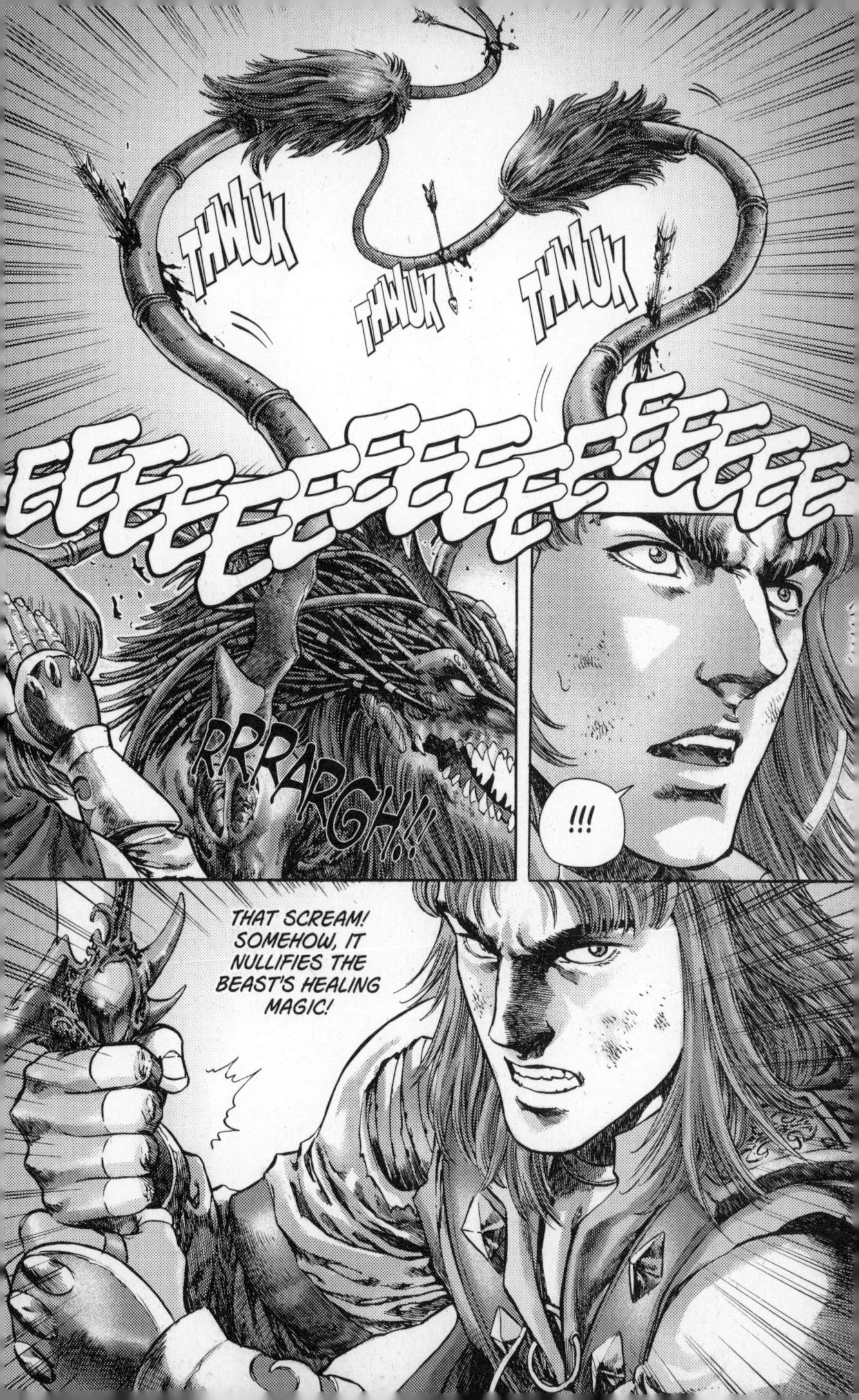
THWUK
THWUK
THWUK
EEEEEEEEEEEEEEEEEEEEEEEEEE
!!!
RRRARGH!!
THAT SCREAM! SOMEHOW, IT NULLIFIES THE BEAST'S HEALING MAGIC!

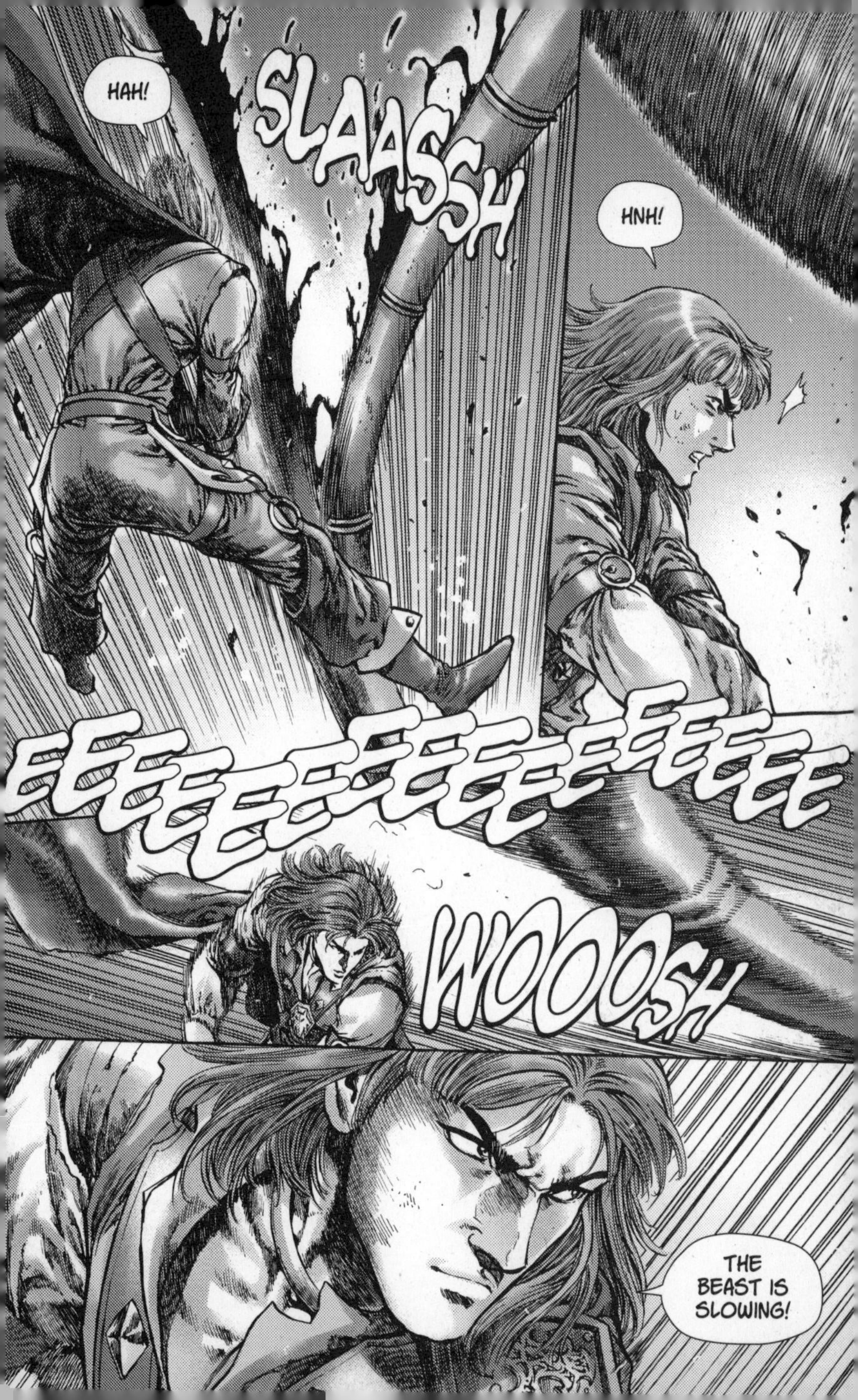
HAH!
SLAASSH
HNH!
EEEEEEEEEEEEEEEEEEEE
WOOOSH
THE BEAST IS SLOWING!

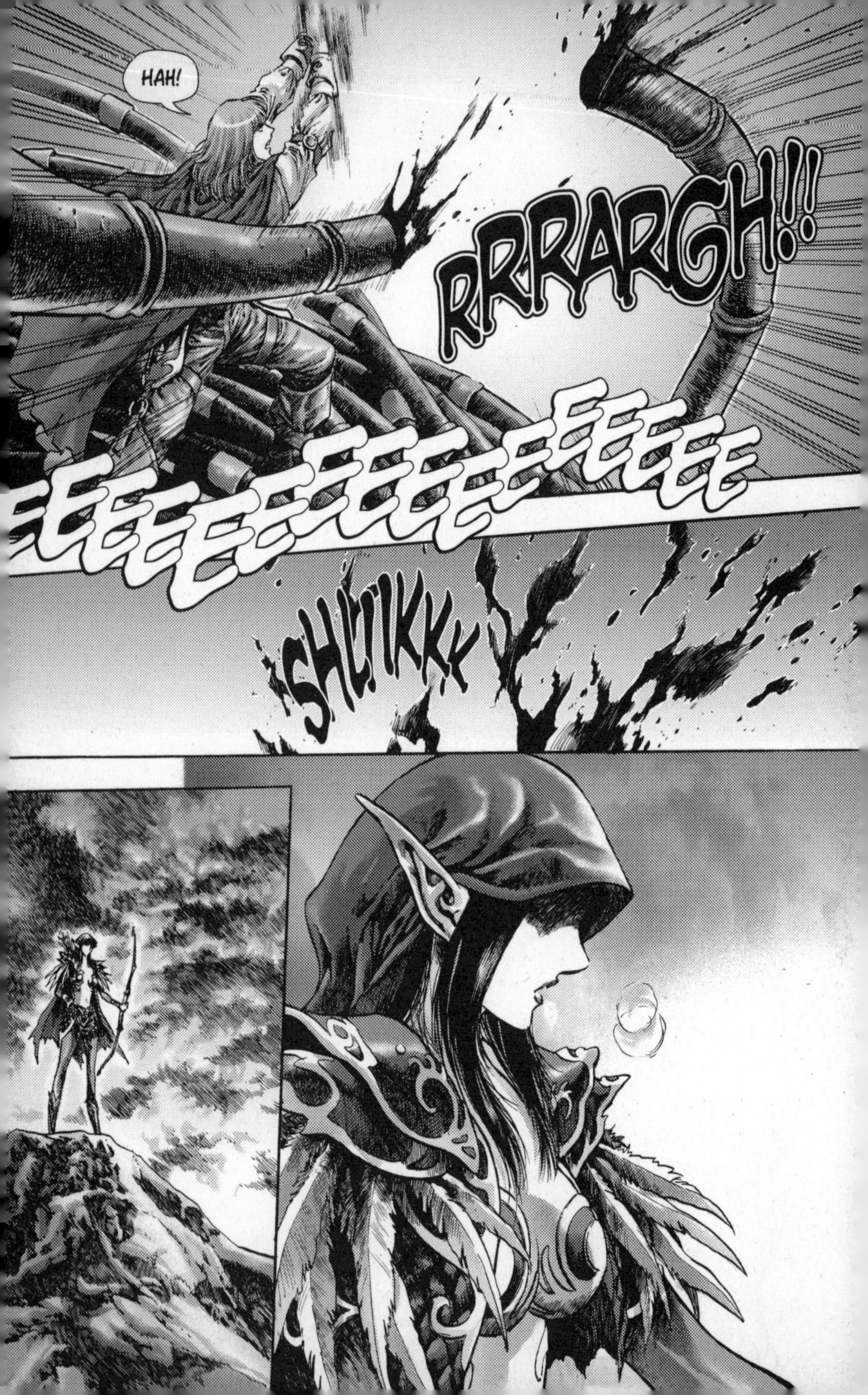

HAH!
RRRARGH!!
EEEEEEEEEEEEEEEEEEEEEEE
SHUIKKK

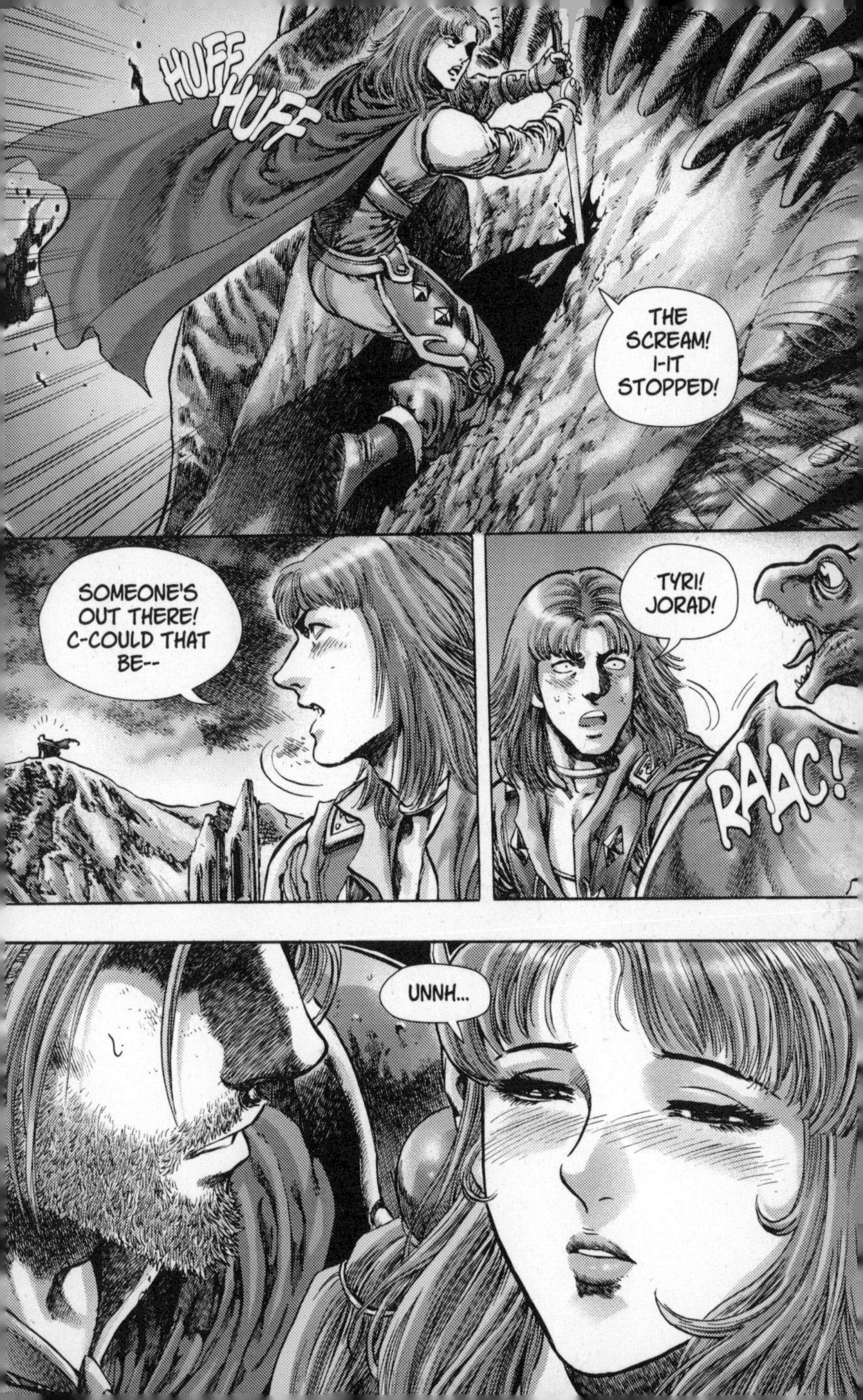
HUFF HUFF
THE SCREAM! I-IT STOPPED!
SOMEONE'S OUT THERE! C-COULD THAT BE--
TYRI! JORAD!
RAAC!
UNNH...

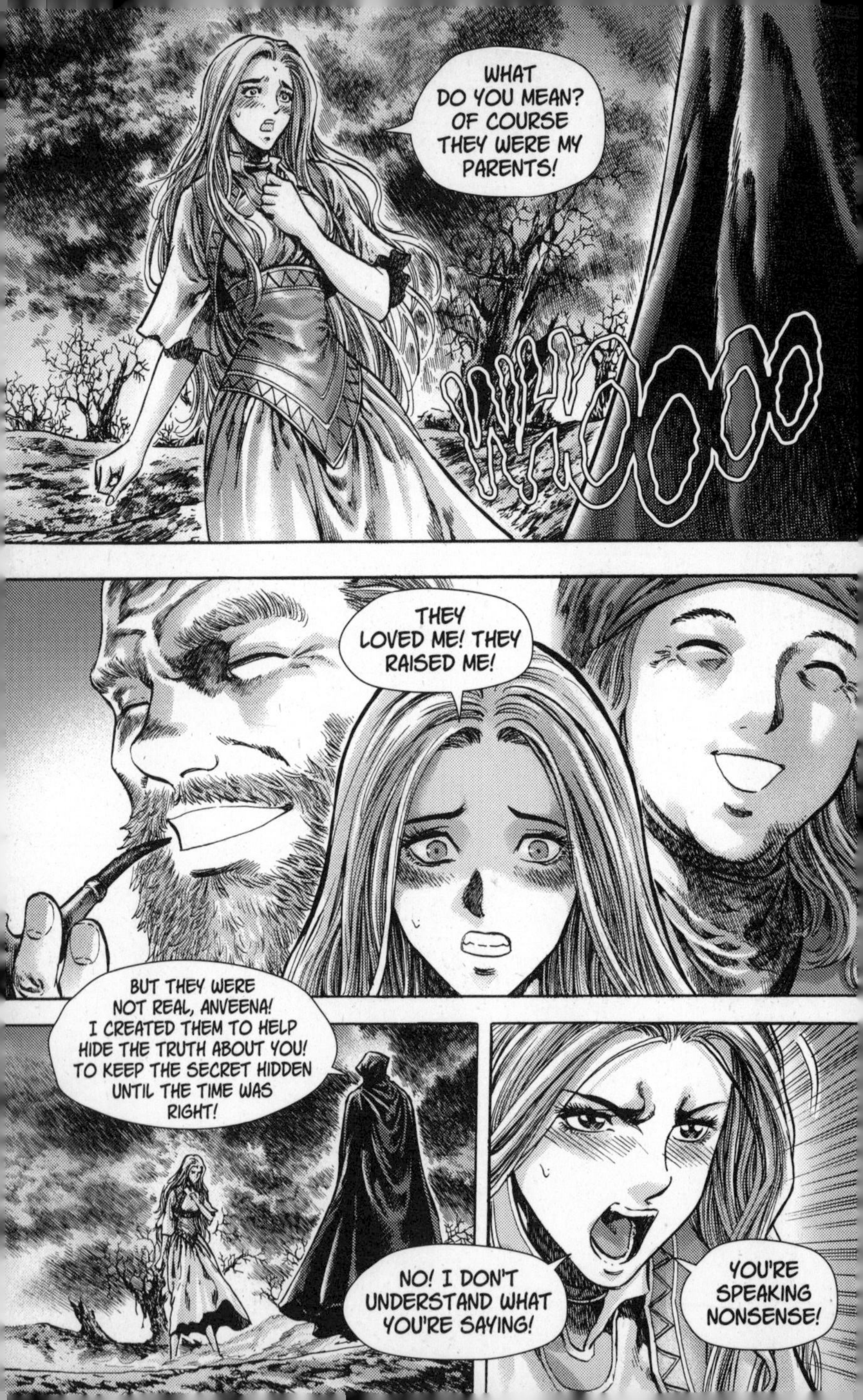
WHAT DO YOU MEAN? OF COURSE THEY WERE MY PARENTS!
WHOOOOO
THEY LOVED ME! THEY RAISED ME!
BUT THEY WERE NOT REAL, ANVEENA! I CREATED THEM TO HELP HIDE THE TRUTH ABOUT YOU! TO KEEP THE SECRET HIDDEN UNTIL THE TIME WAS RIGHT!
NO! I DON'T UNDERSTAND WHAT YOU'RE SAYING!
YOU'RE SPEAKING NONSENSE!

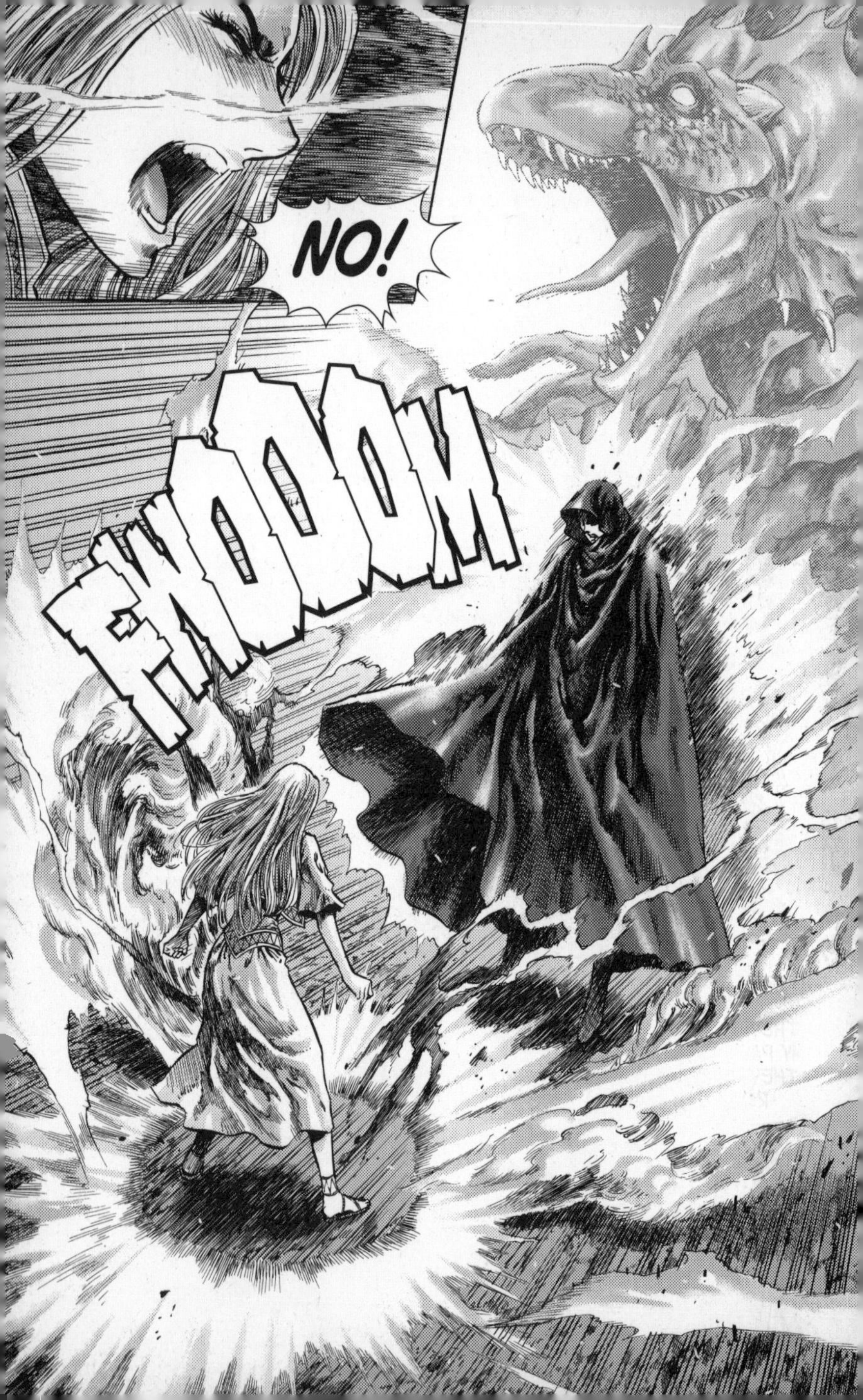
NO!
FWOOOM

CHAPTER FOUR
DARK REUNION

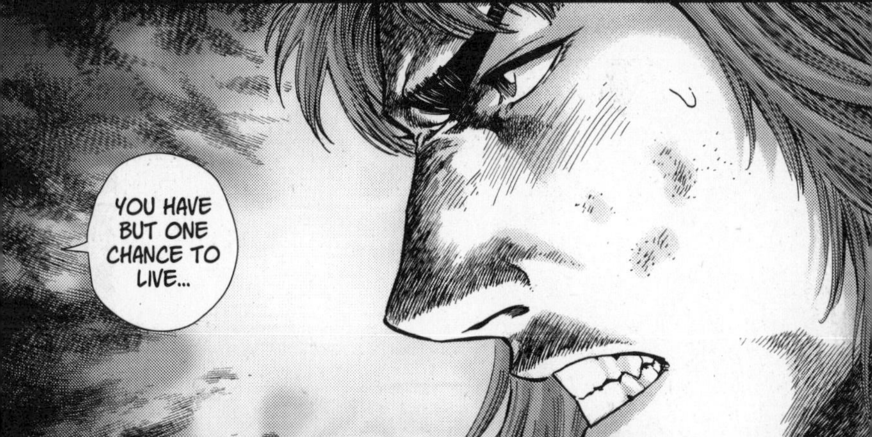

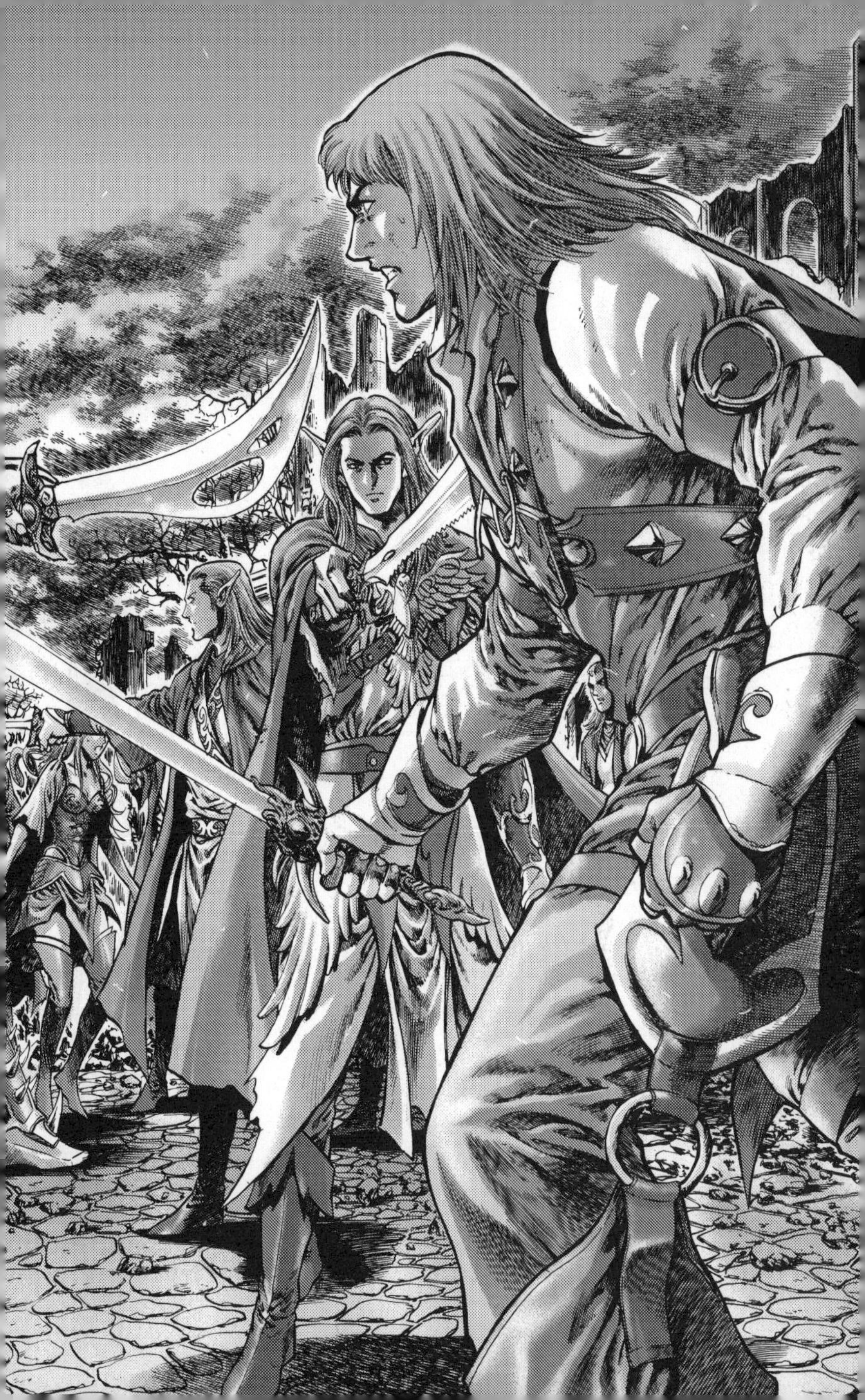

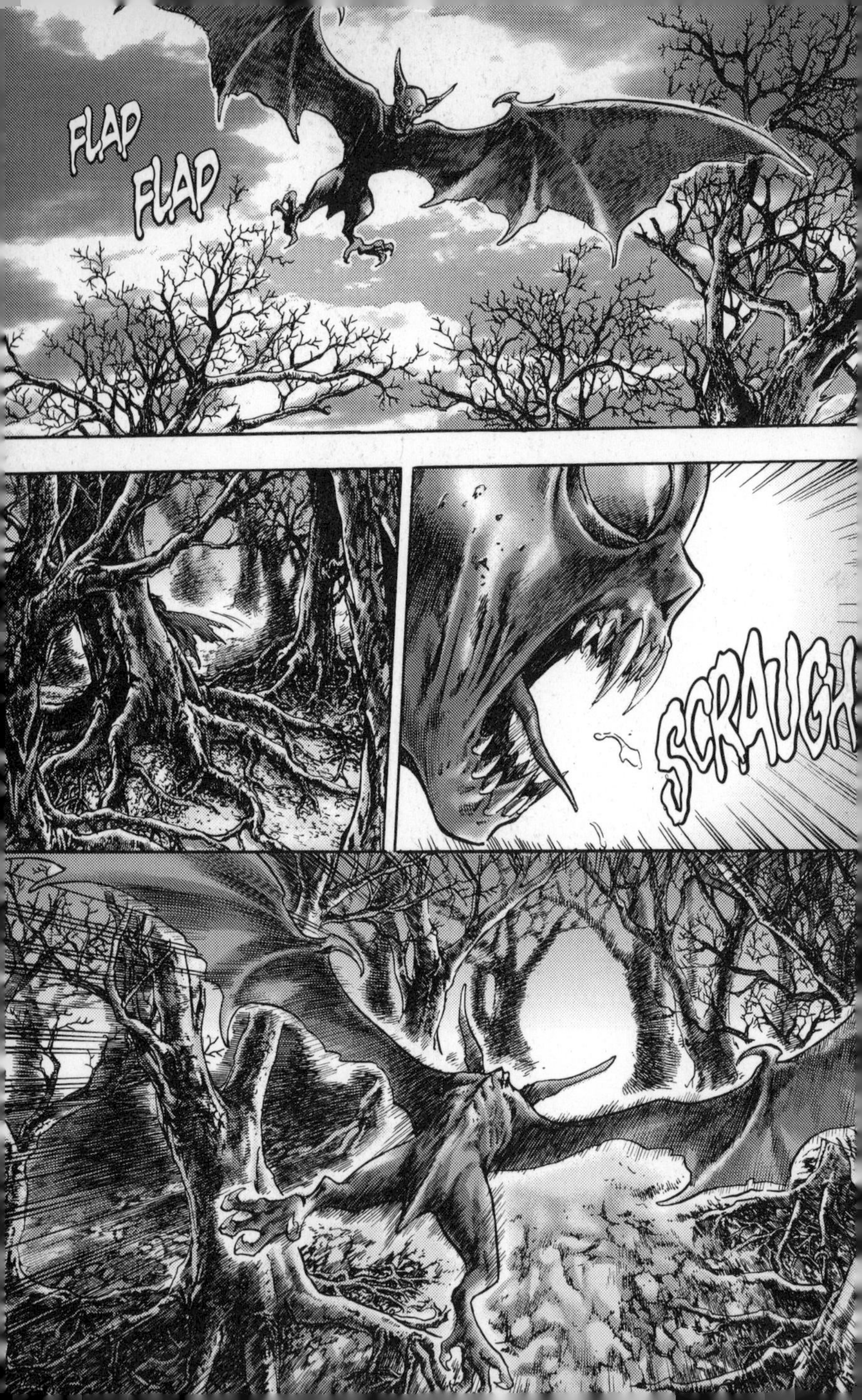
FLAP
FLAP
SCRAUGH

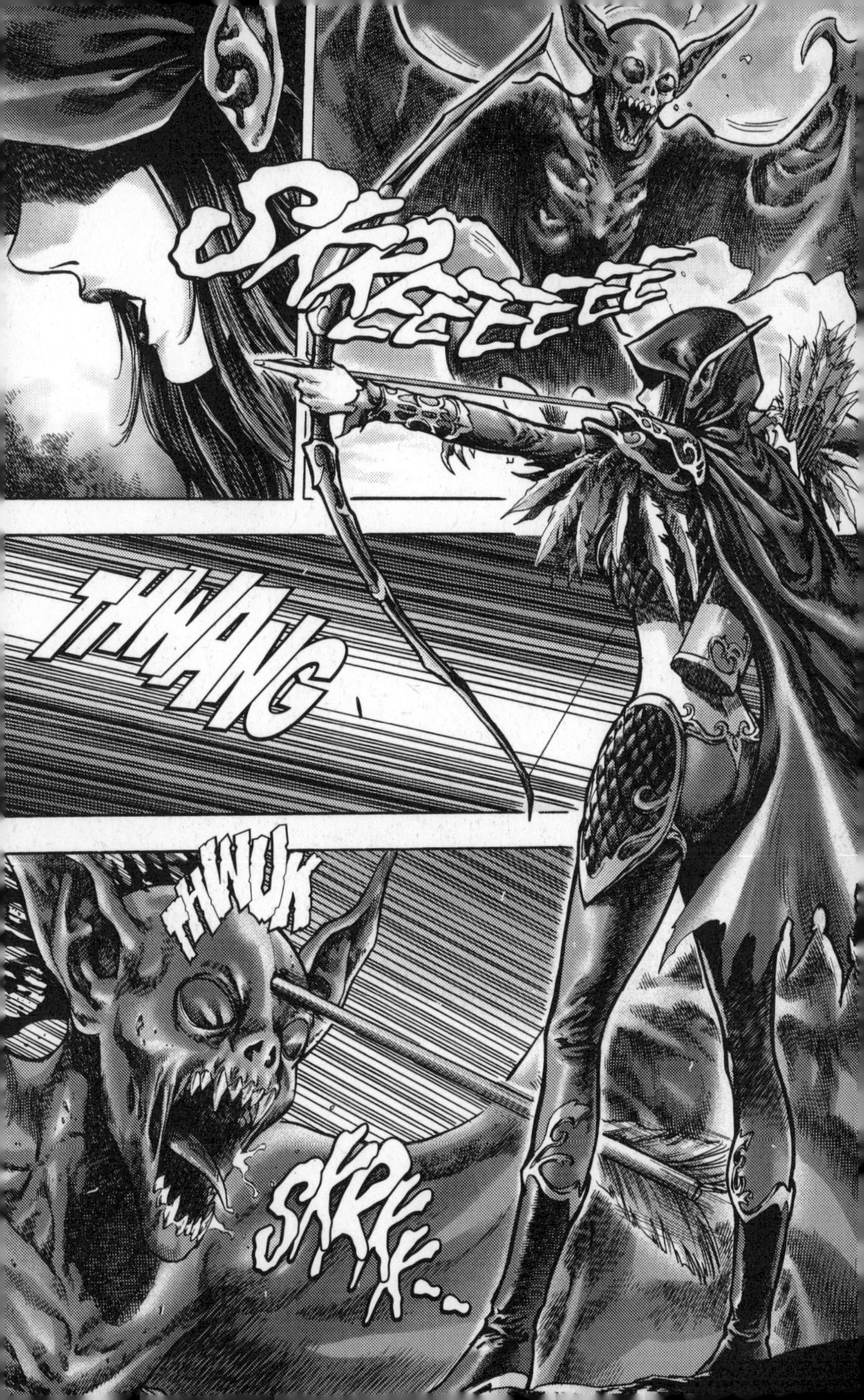
SKREEEEEEE
THWANG
THWUK
SKRKK--

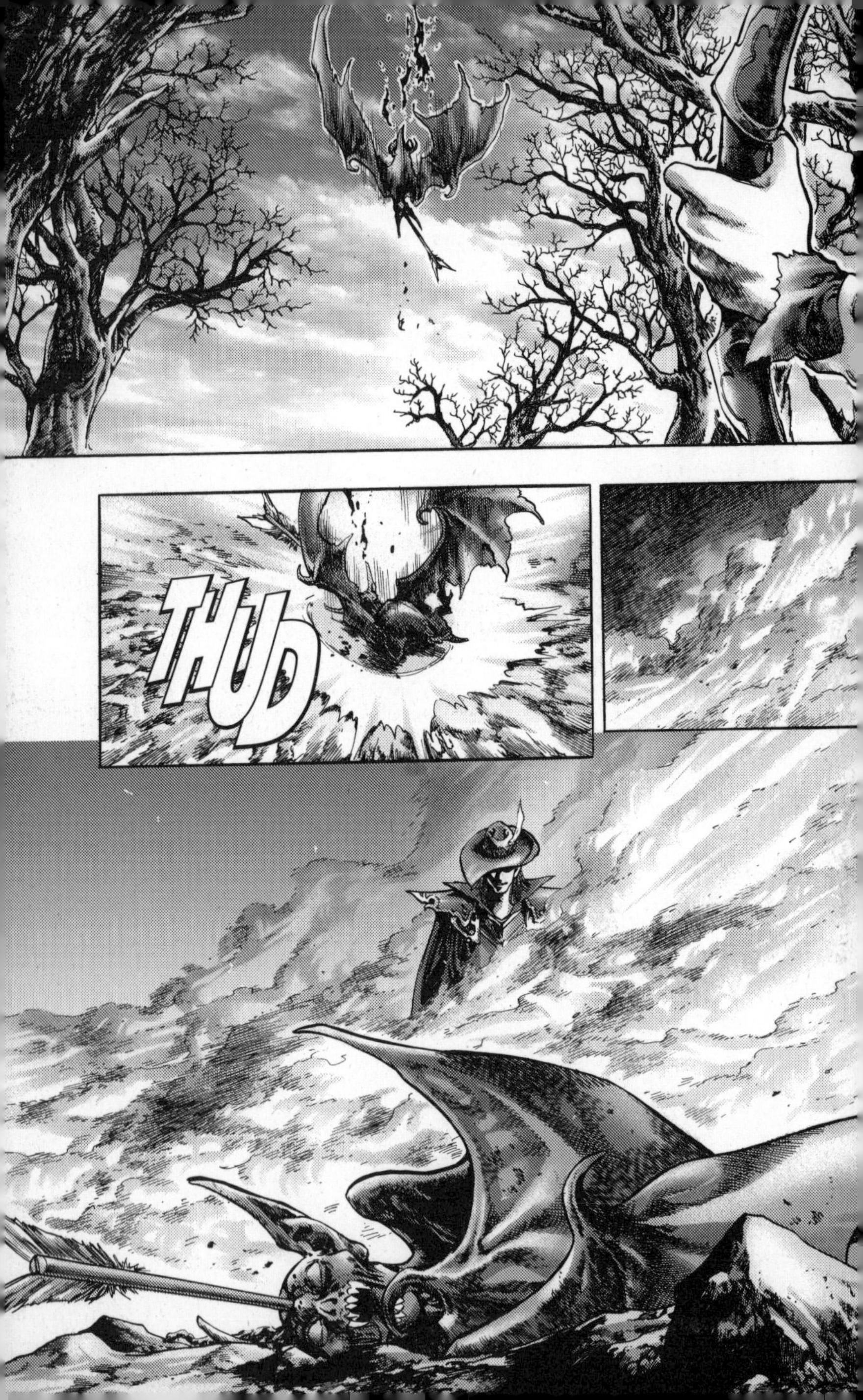
THUD

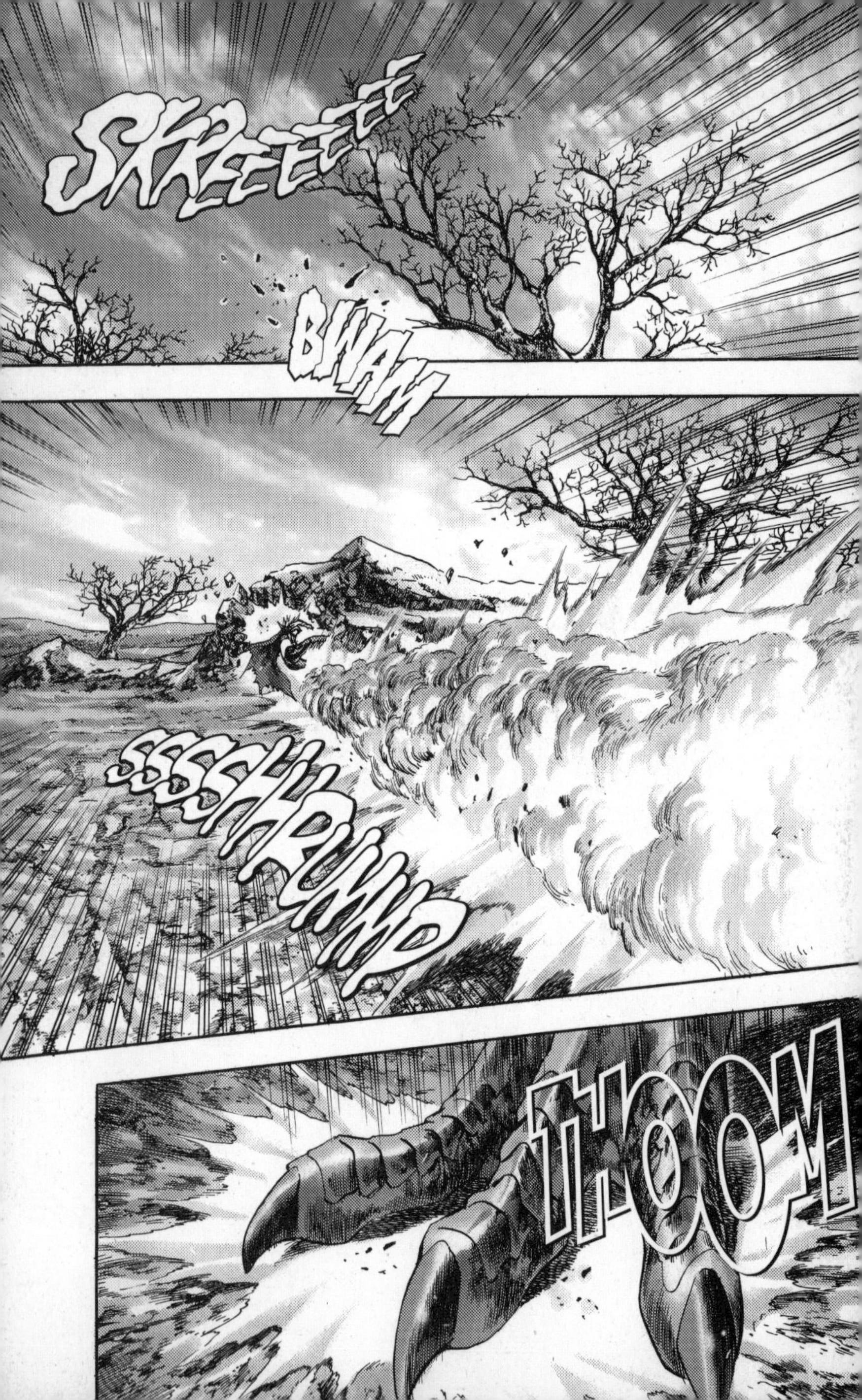
SKREEEEEE
BWAM
SSSCHRUMMP
THOOM

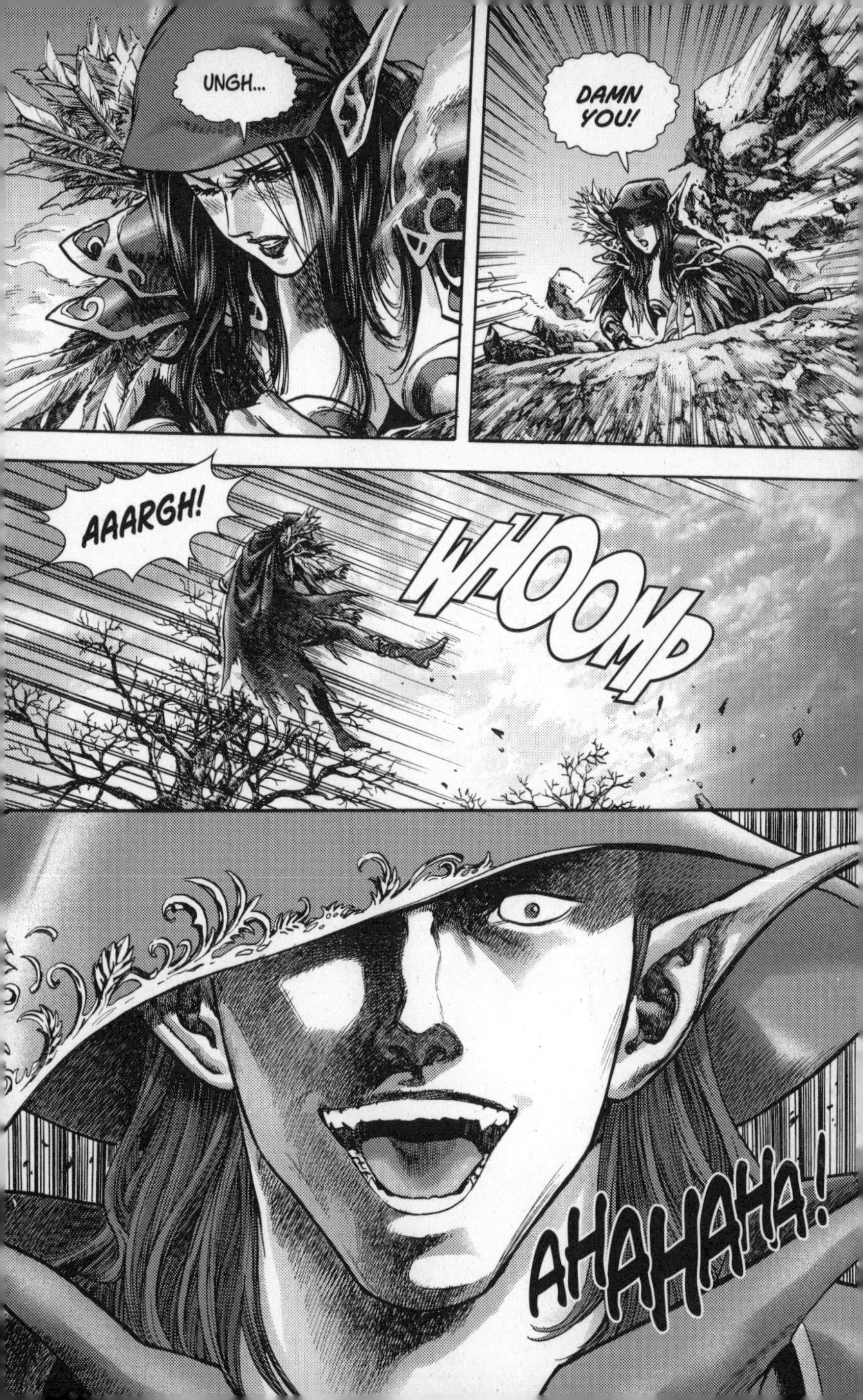
UNGH...
DAMN YOU!
AAARGH!
WHOOMP
AHAHAHA!

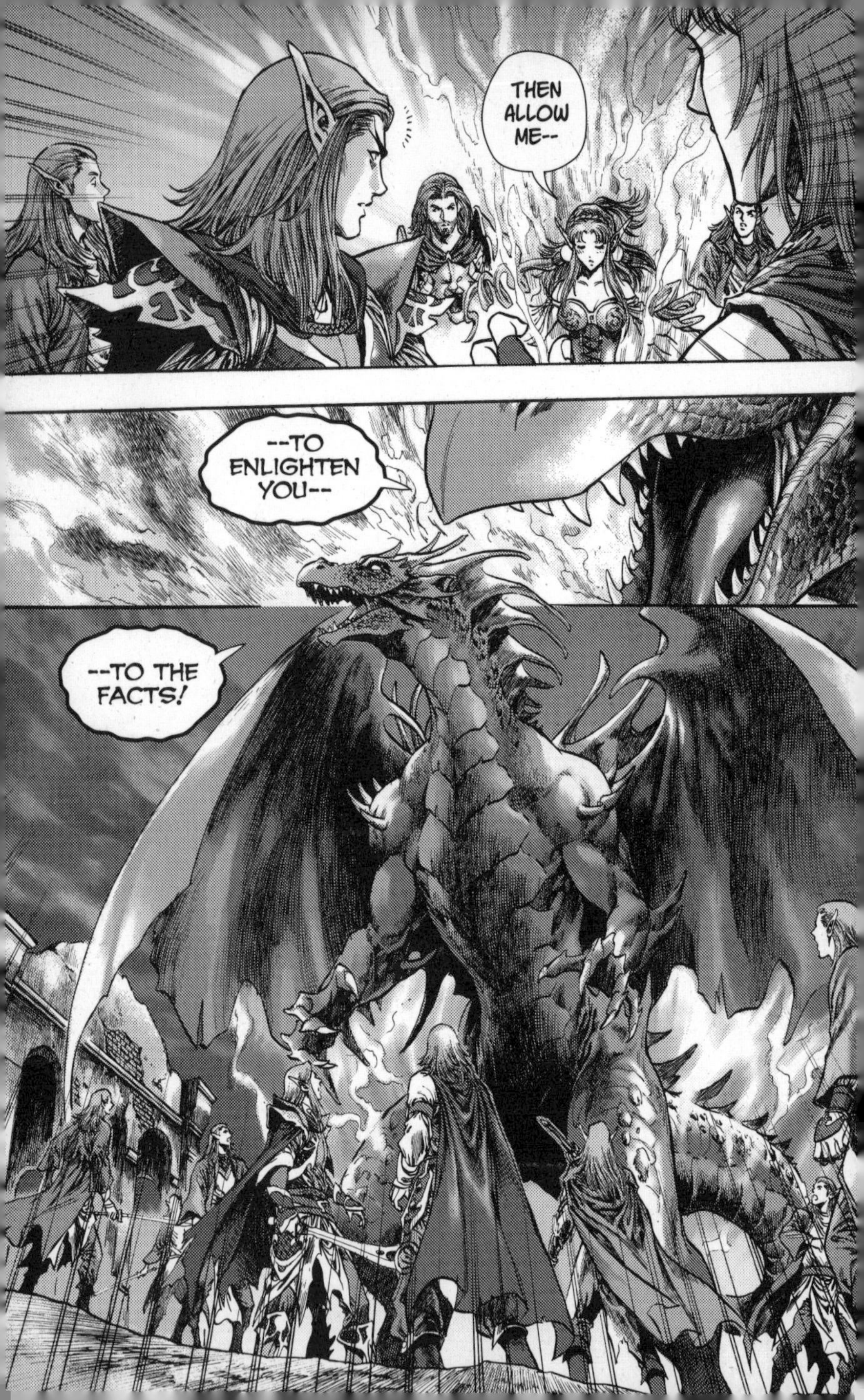
THEN ALLOW ME--
--TO ENLIGHTEN YOU--
--TO THE FACTS!

CHAPTER FIVE
EDGE OF THE ABYSS

THERE! WE MUST LAND THERE!

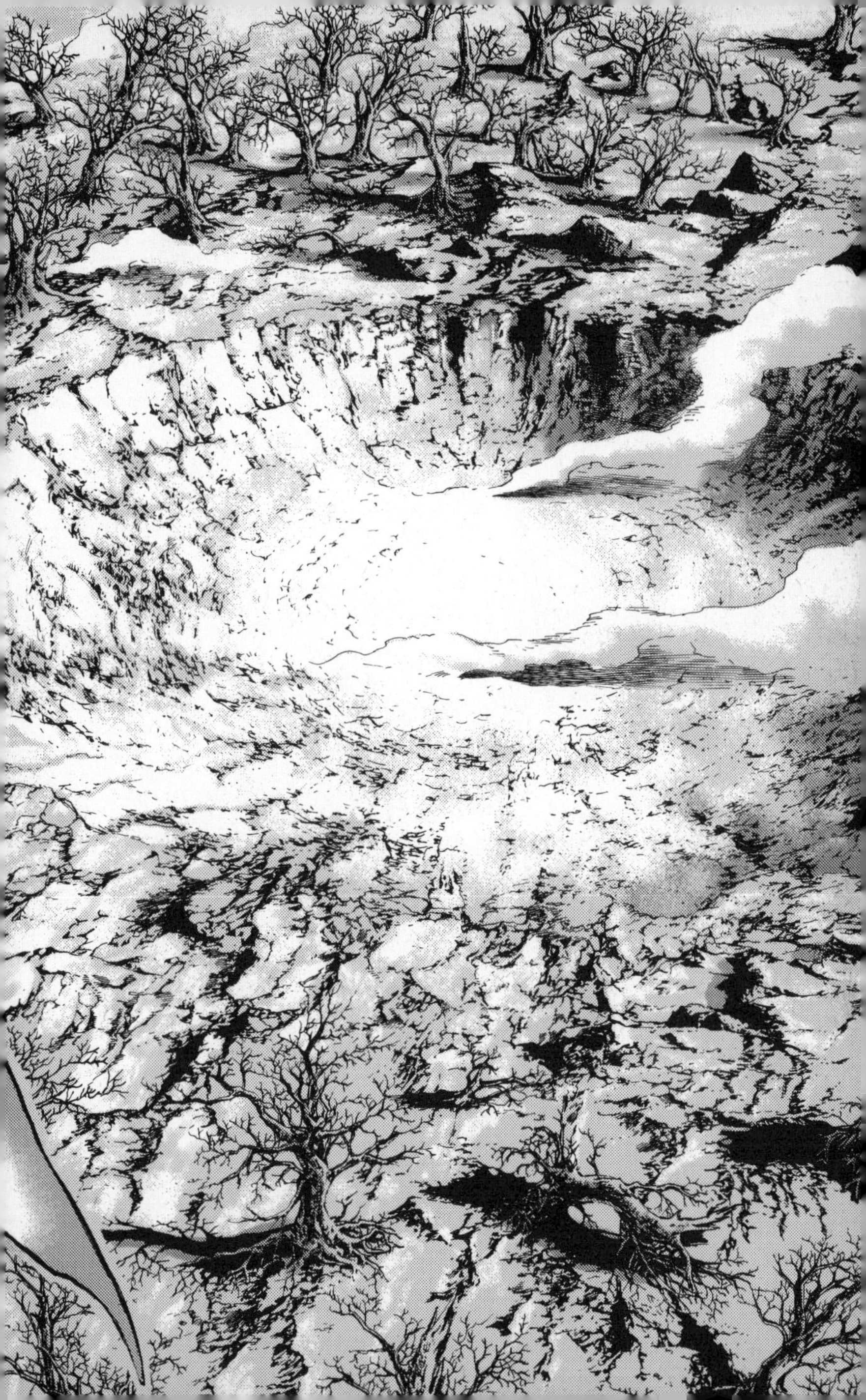

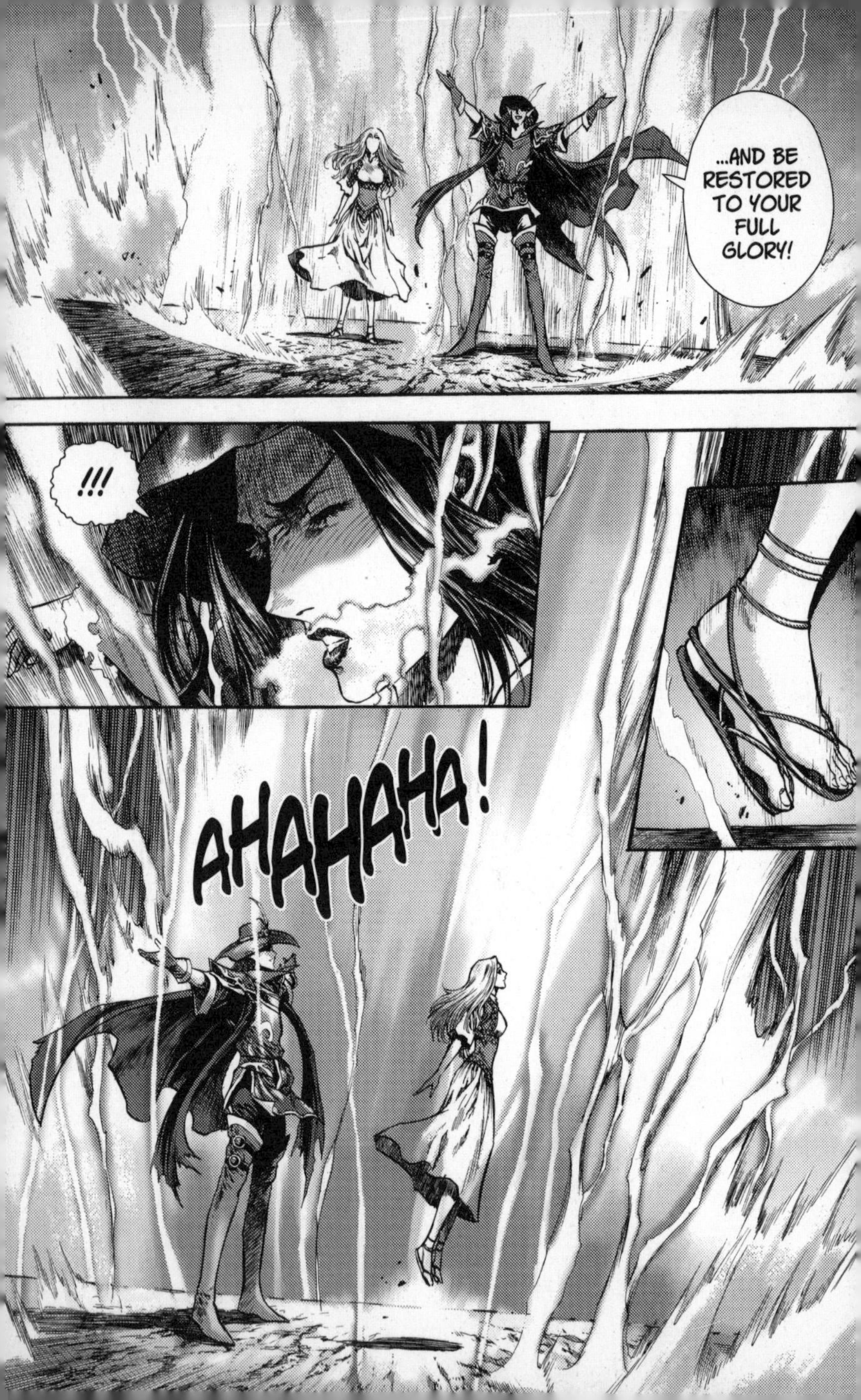
...AND BE RESTORED TO YOUR FULL GLORY!
!!!
AHAHAHA!

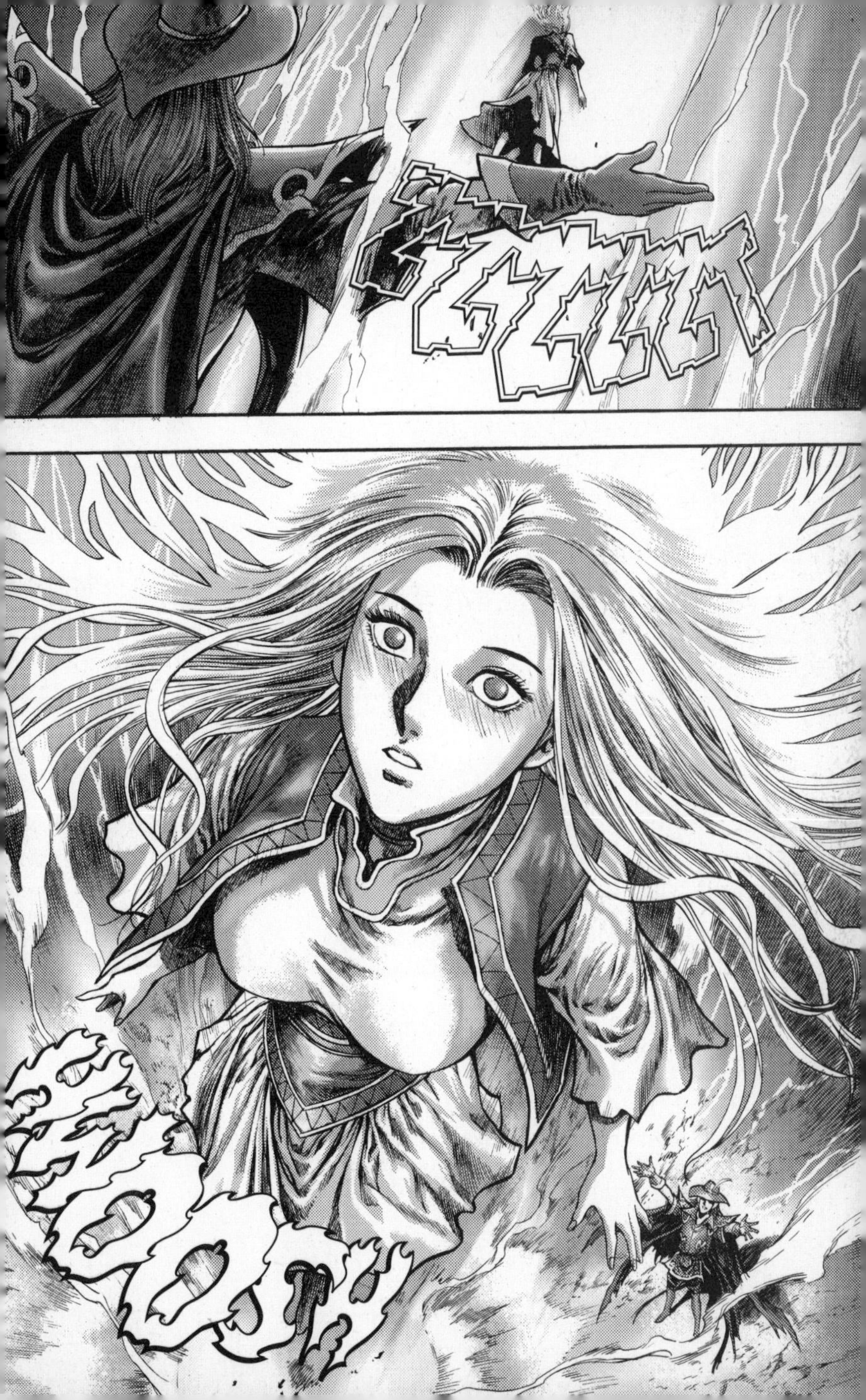

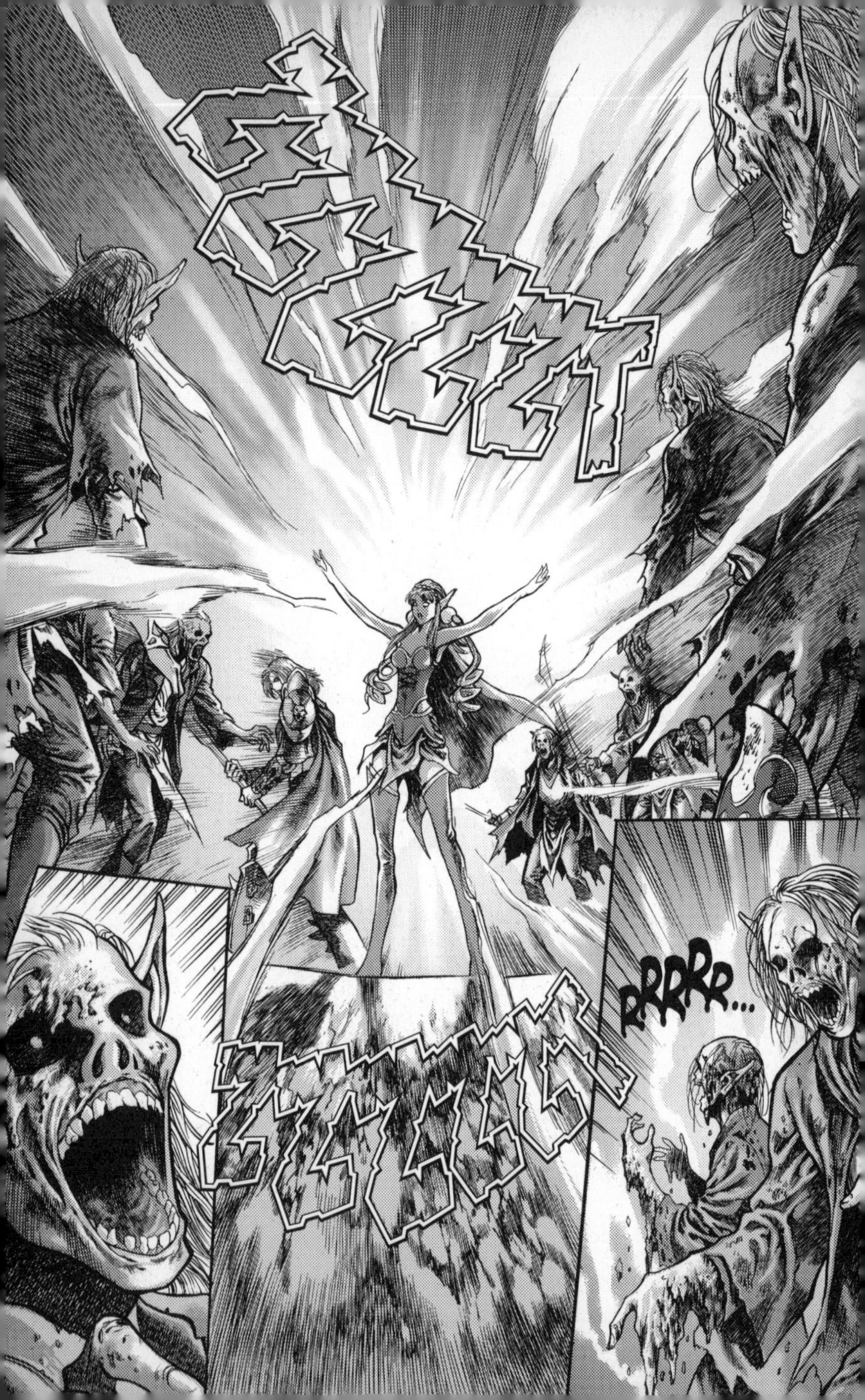
RRRRR...

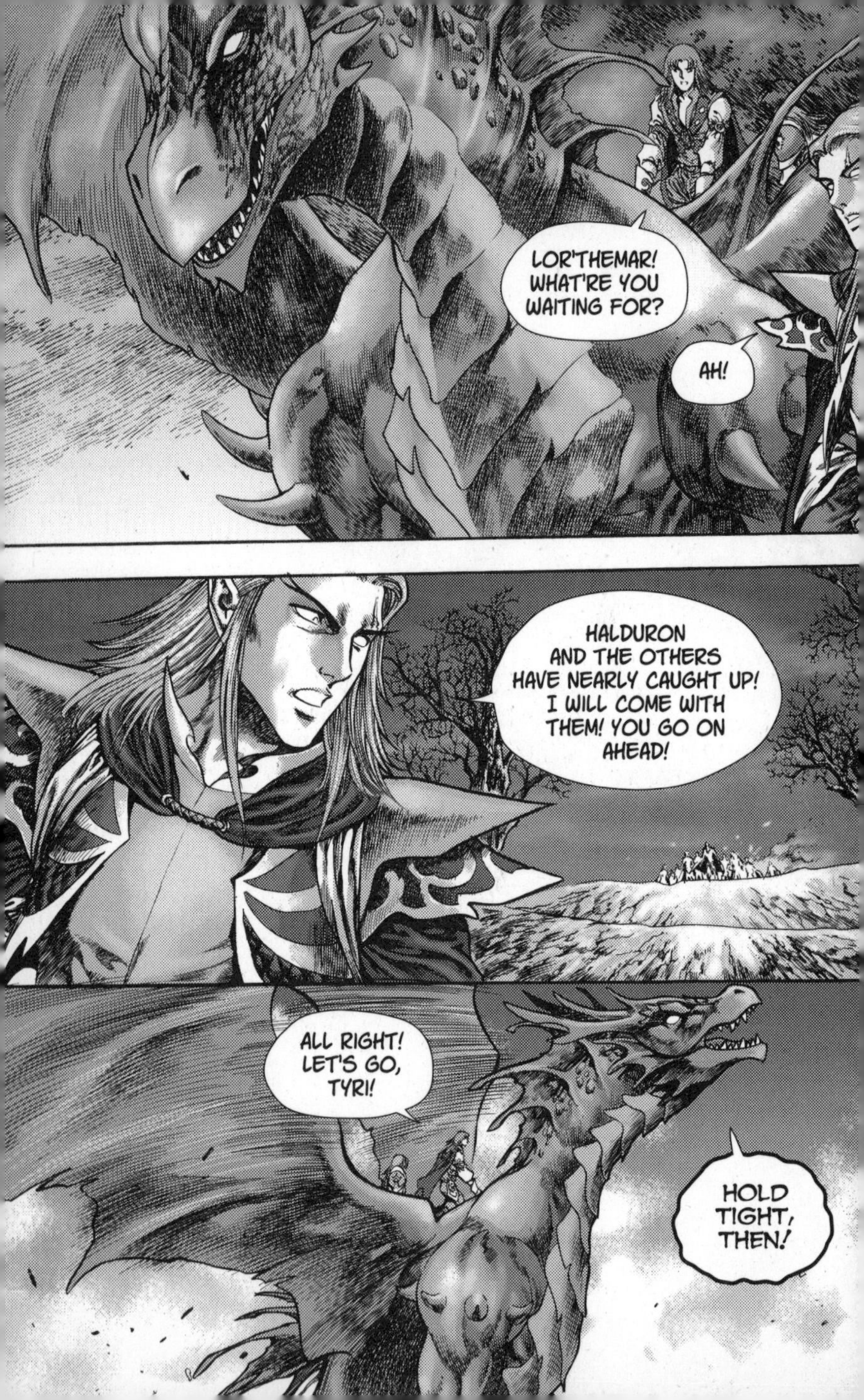
LOR'THEMAR! WHAT'RE YOU WAITING FOR?
AH!
HALDURON AND THE OTHERS HAVE NEARLY CAUGHT UP! I WILL COME WITH THEM! YOU GO ON AHEAD!
ALL RIGHT! LET'S GO, TYRI!
HOLD TIGHT, THEN!

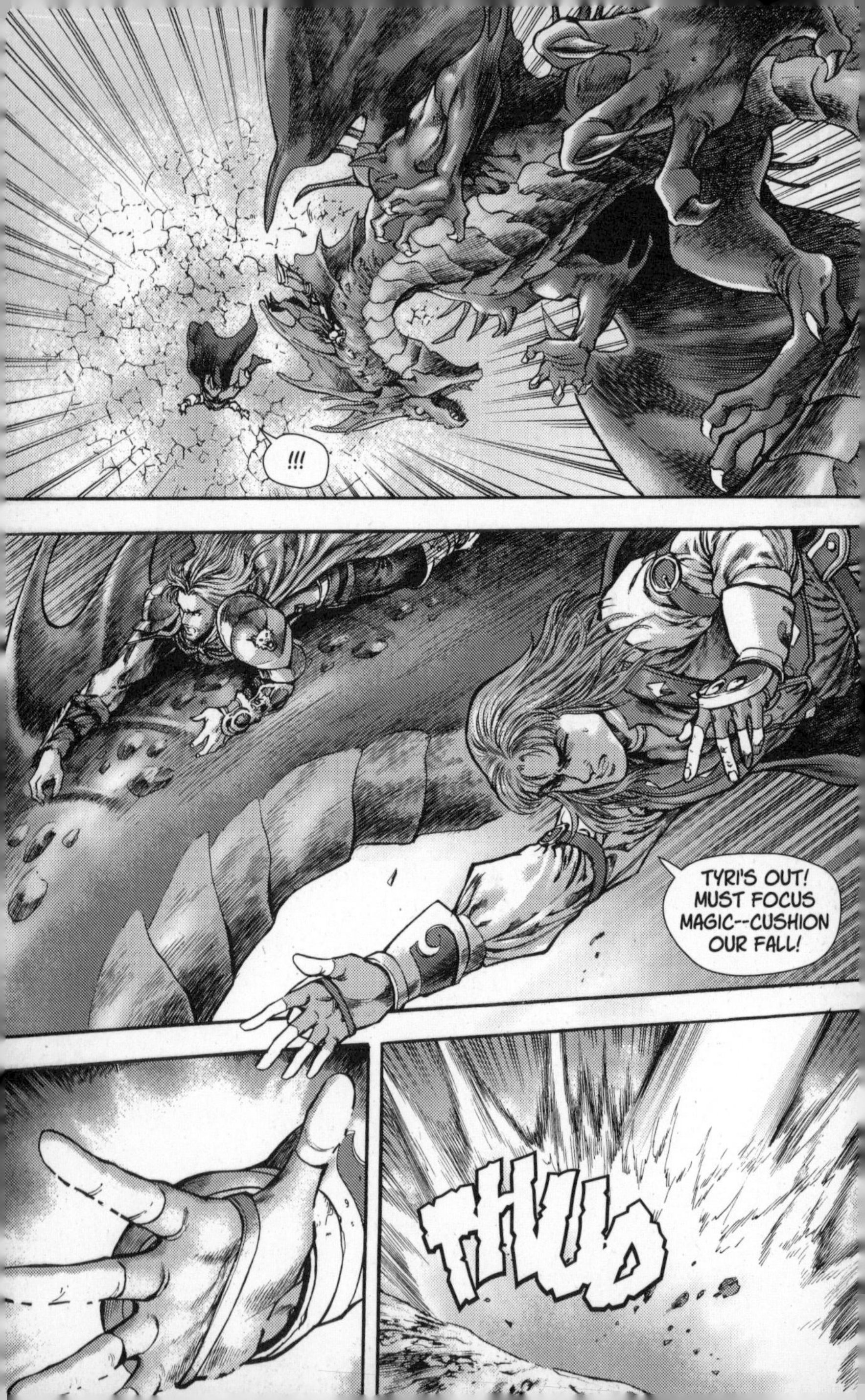
!!!
TYRI'S OUT! MUST FOCUS MAGIC--CUSHION OUR FALL!
THUD

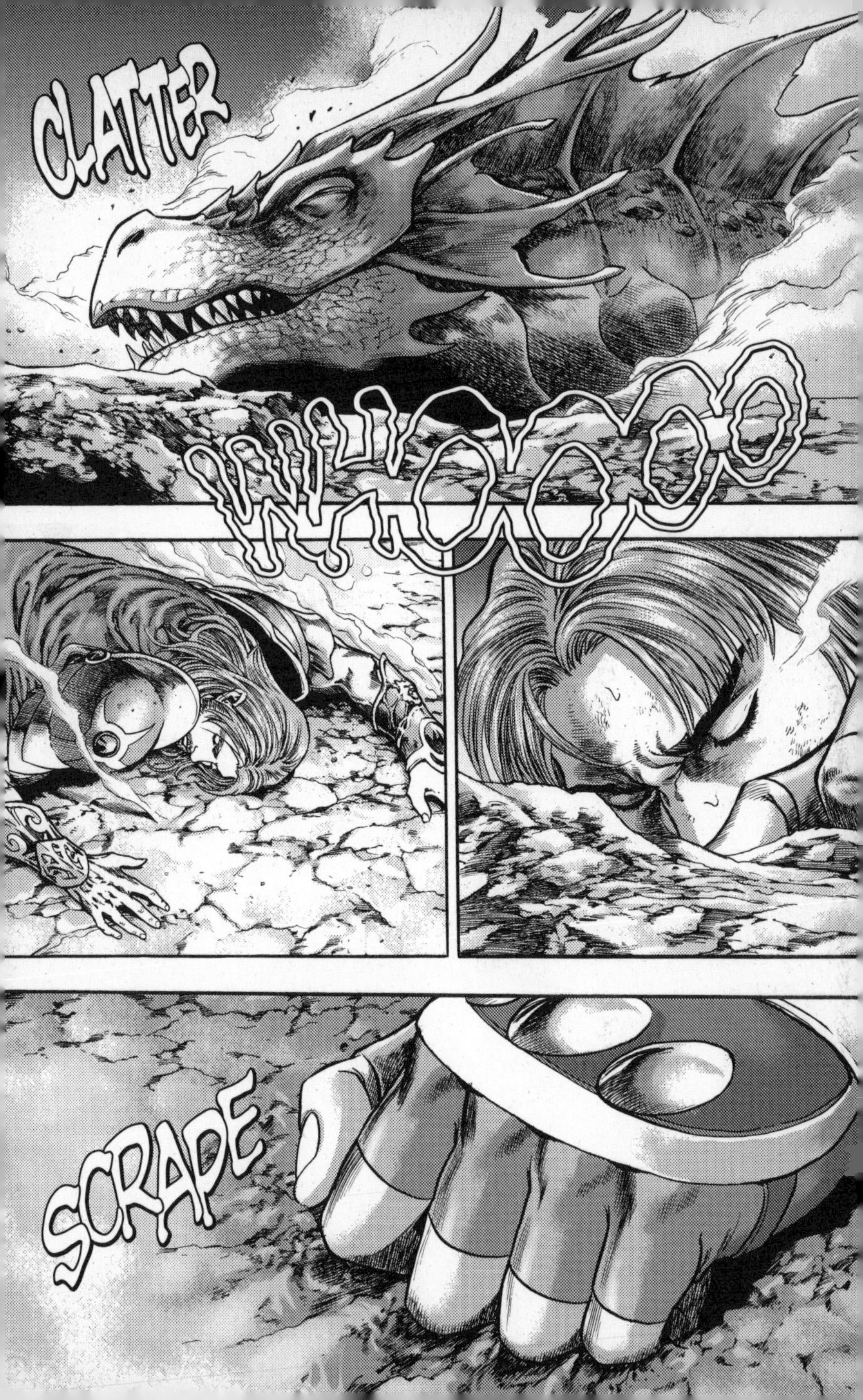
CLATTER
WHOOOOO
SCRAPE

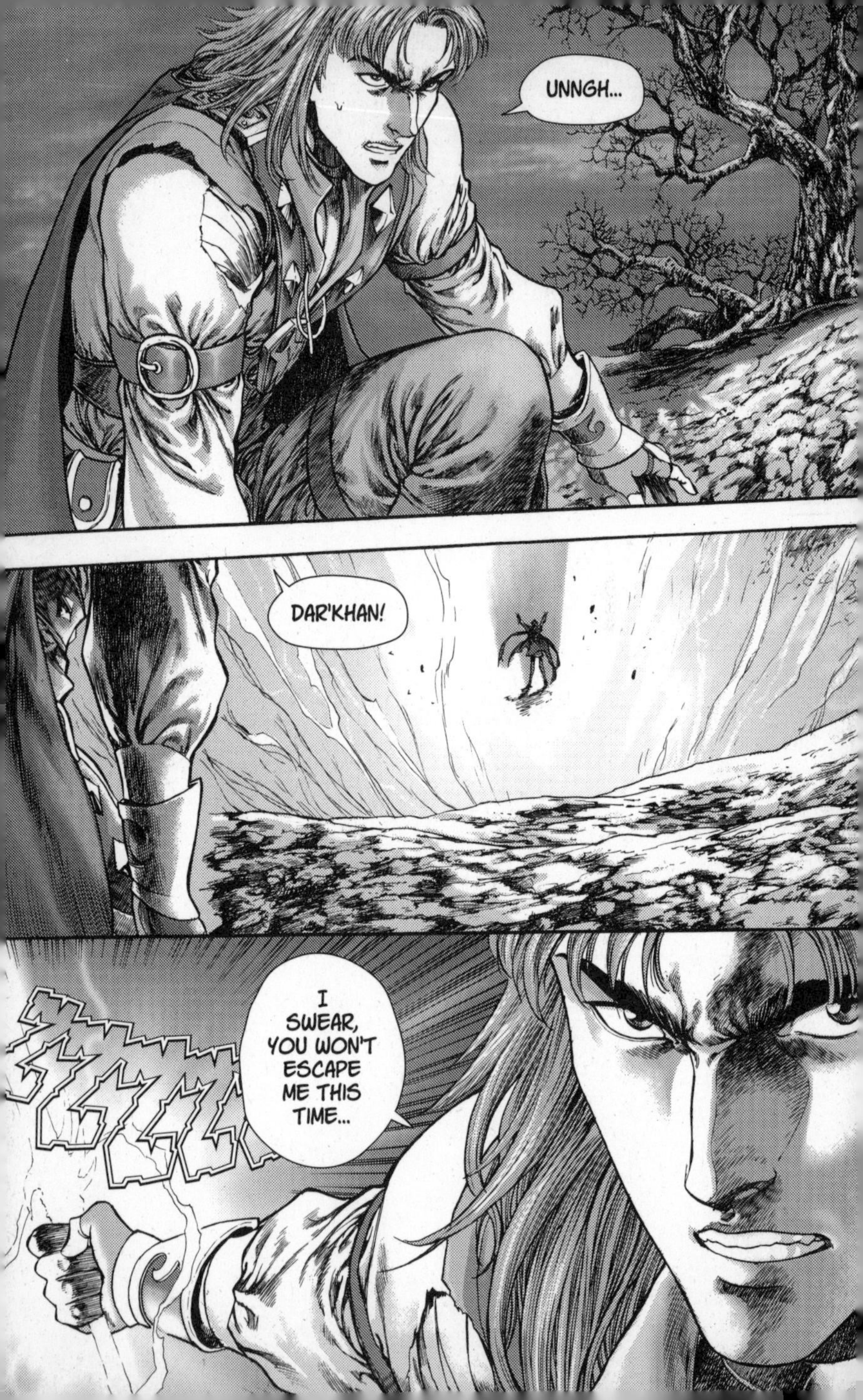
UNNGH...
DAR'KHAN!
I SWEAR, YOU WON'T ESCAPE ME THIS TIME...

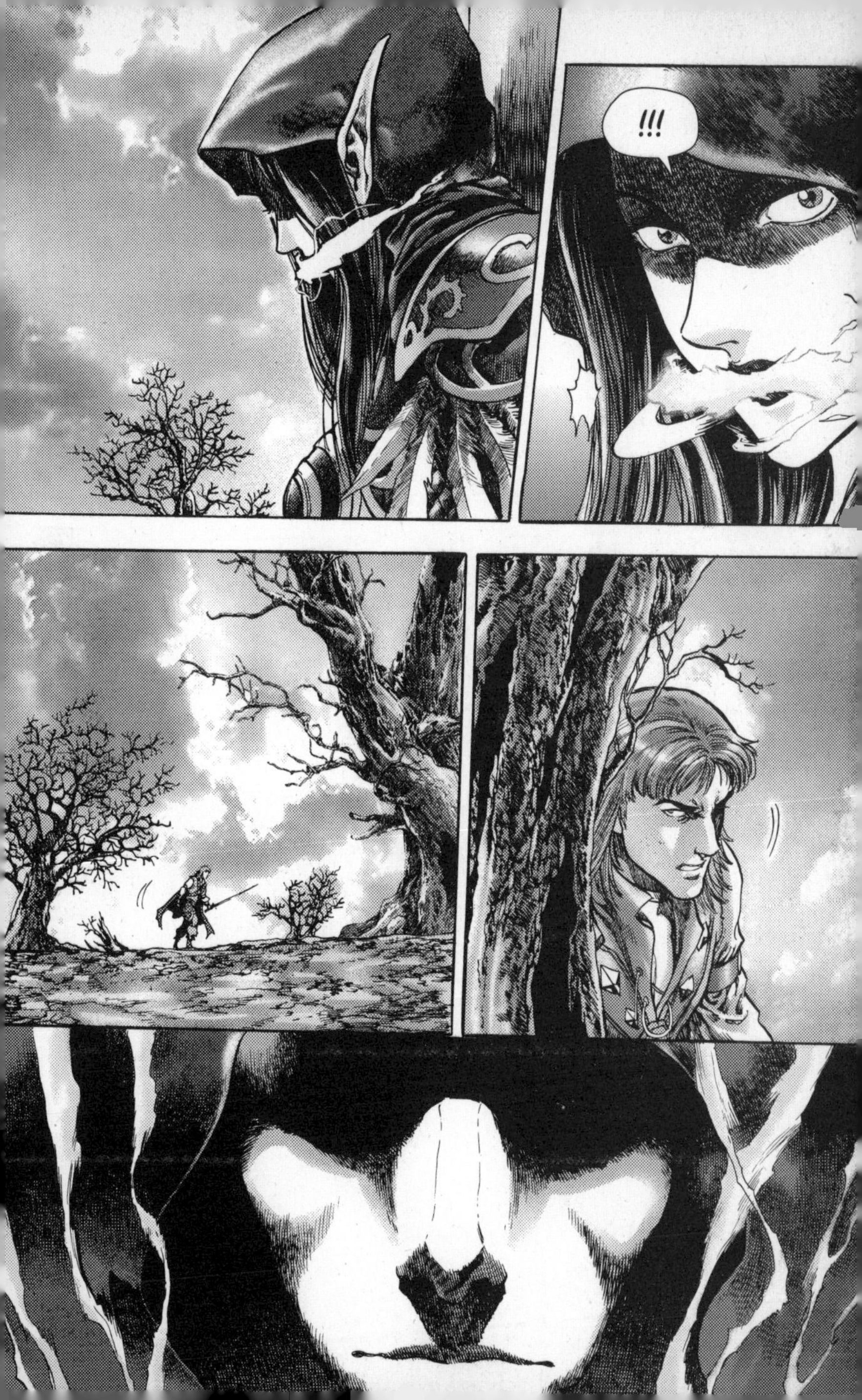
!!!

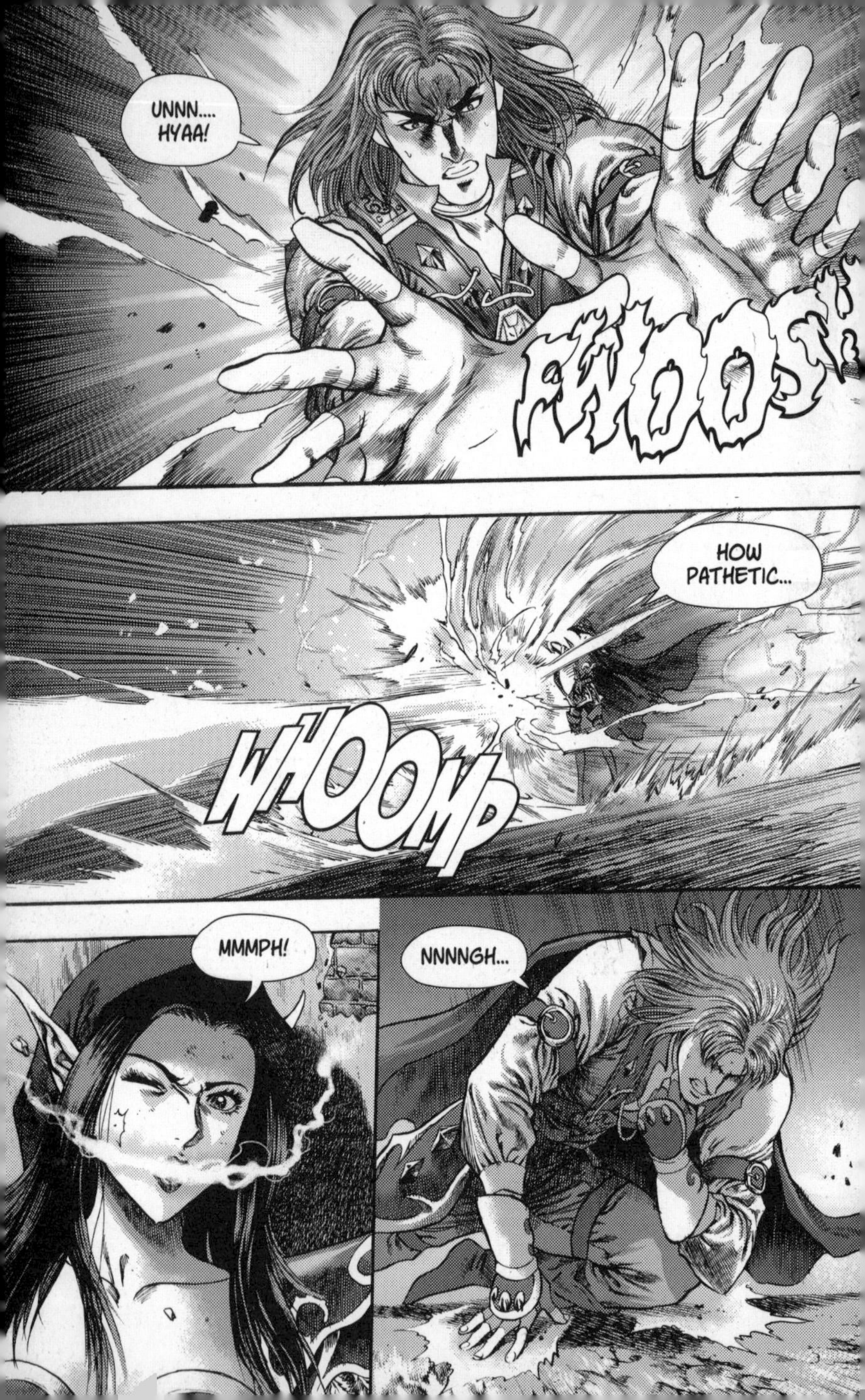
UNNN.... HYAA!
FWOOSH!
HOW PATHETIC...
WHOOMP
MMMPH!
NNNNGH...

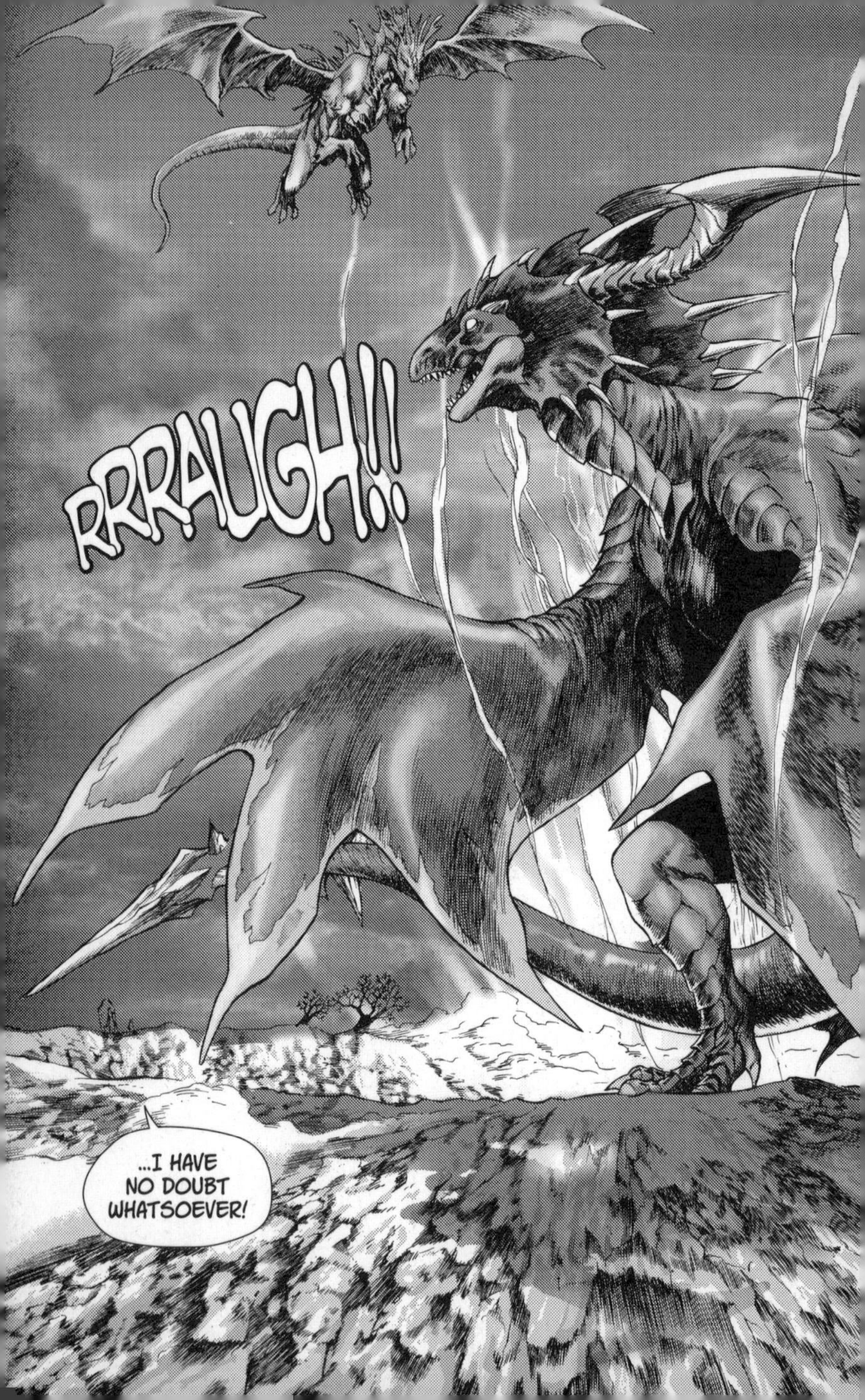
RRRAUGH!!!
...I HAVE NO DOUBT WHATSOEVER!

CHAPTER SIX

FIRE AND FURY

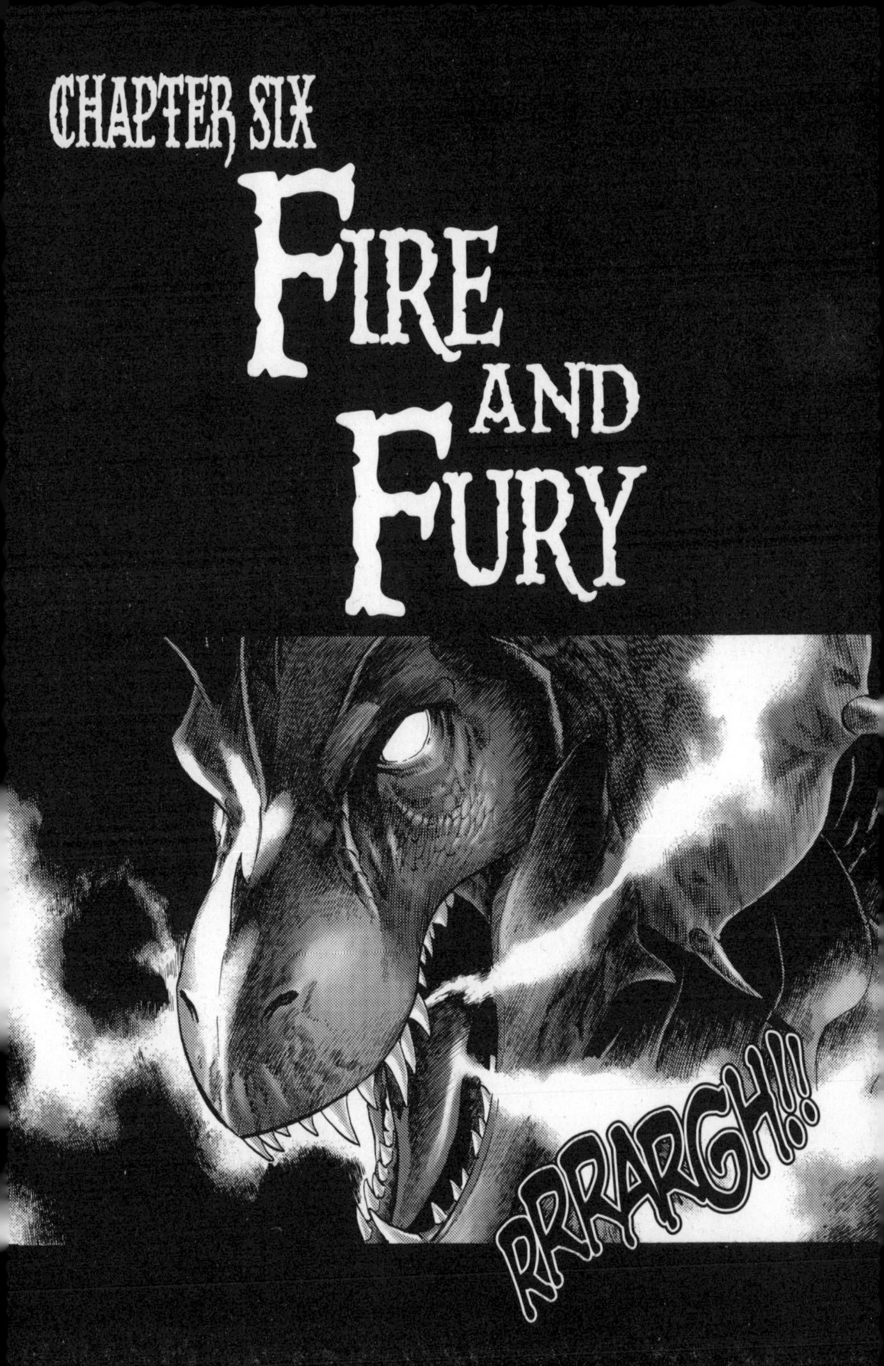
RRRARGH!!!

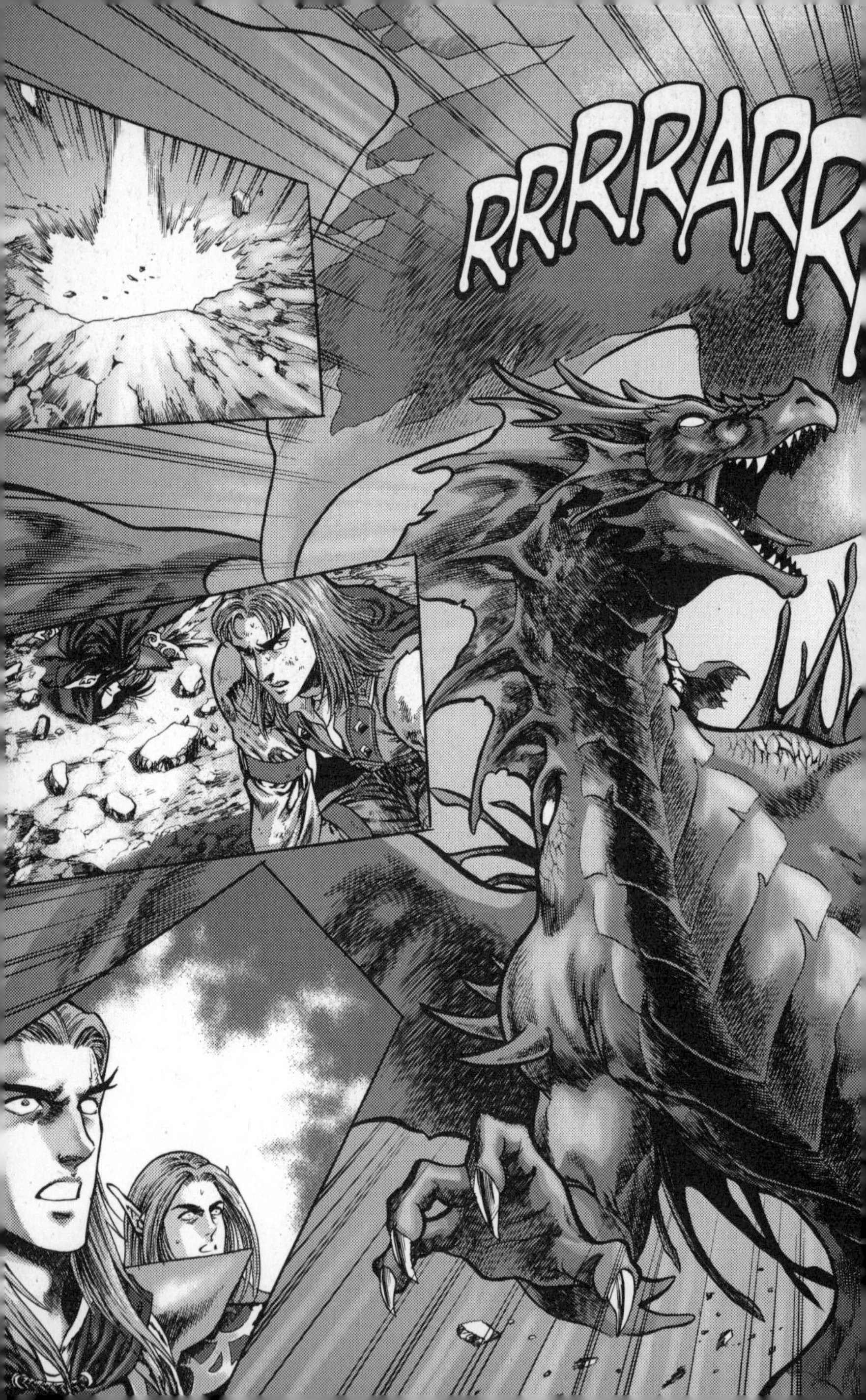
RRRRARR

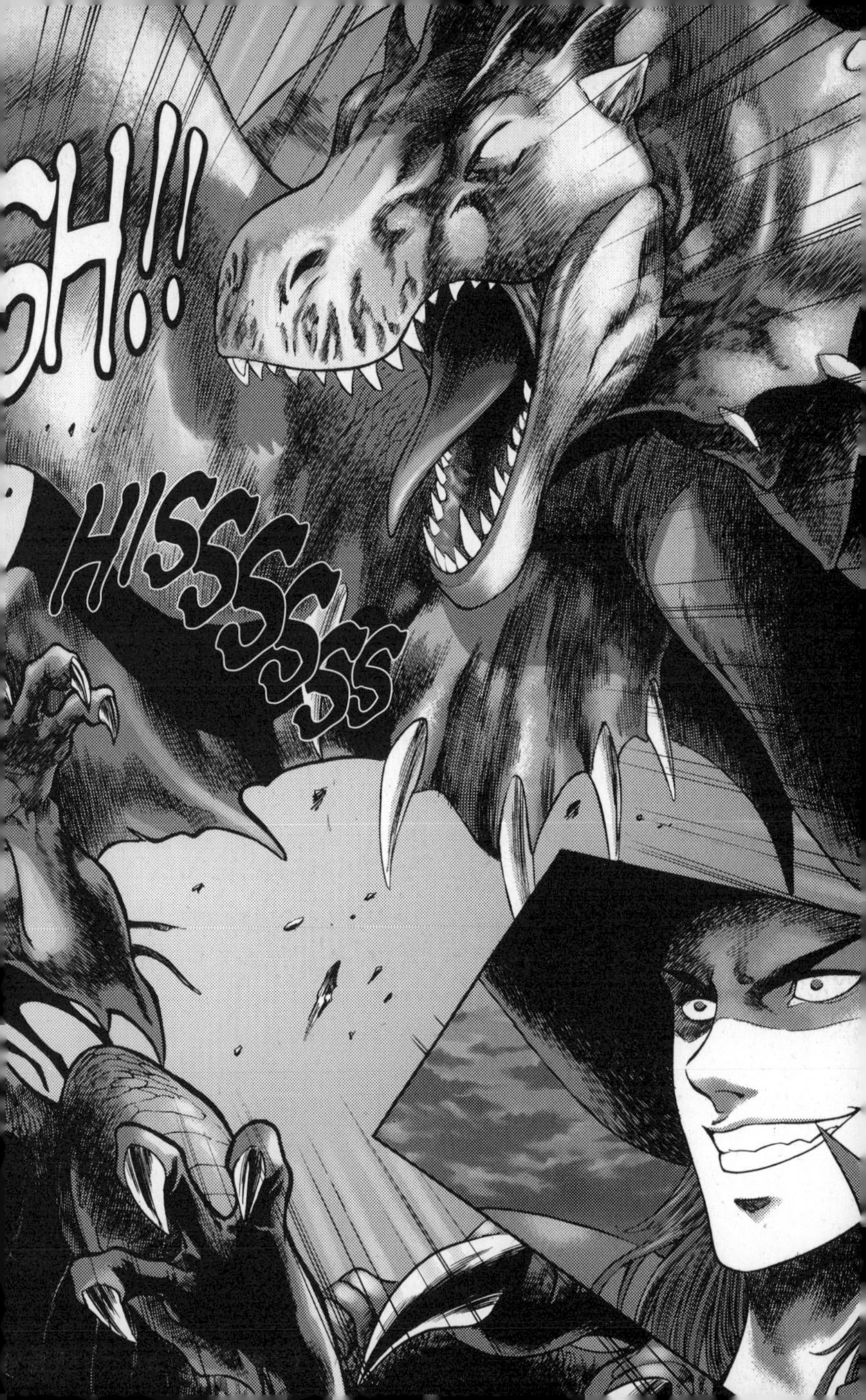

...SH!!
HISSSSSSS

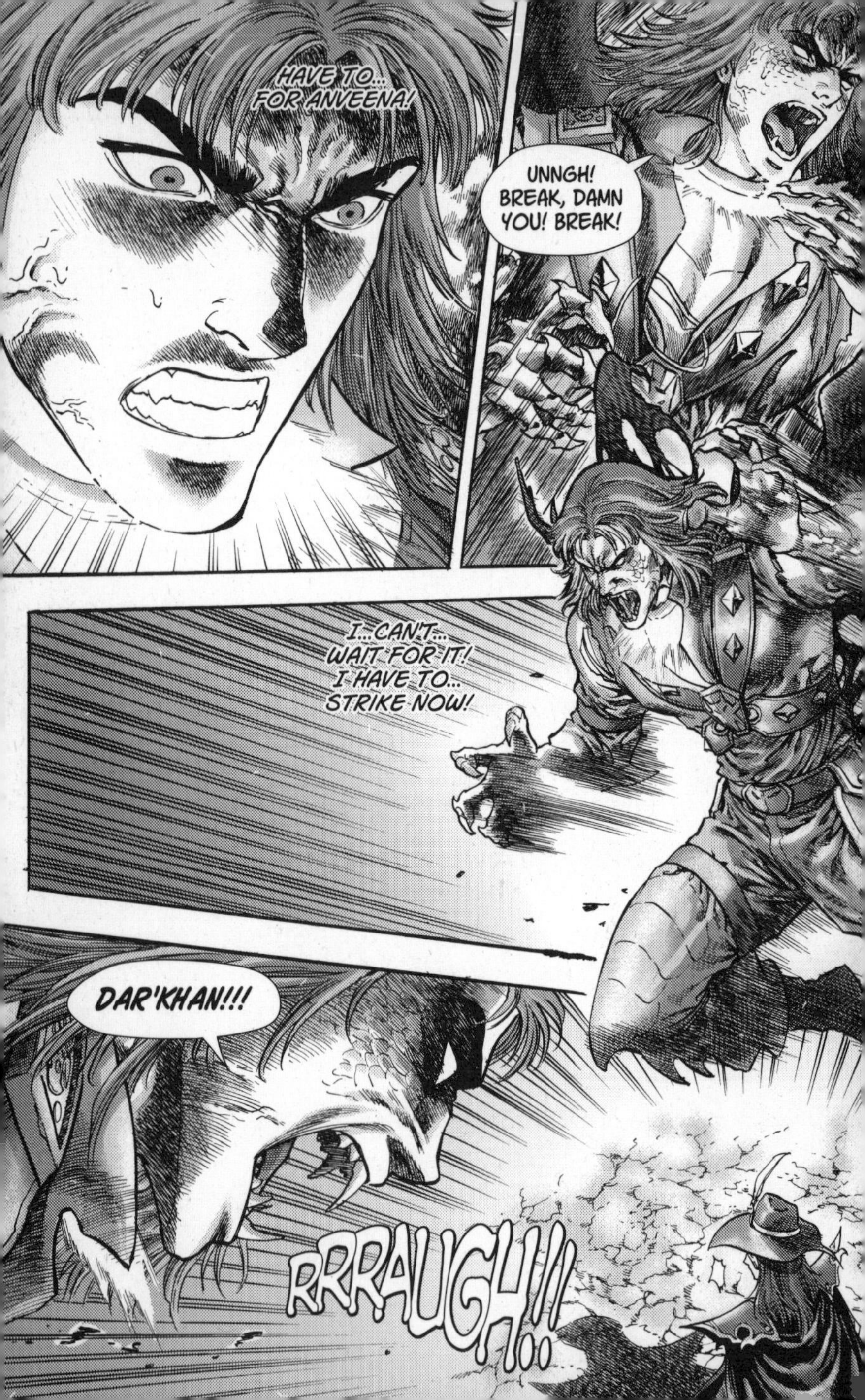
HAVE TO... FOR ANVEENA!
UNNGH! BREAK, DAMN YOU! BREAK!
I...CAN'T... WAIT FOR IT! I HAVE TO... STRIKE NOW!
DAR'KHAN!!!
RRRAUGH!!!

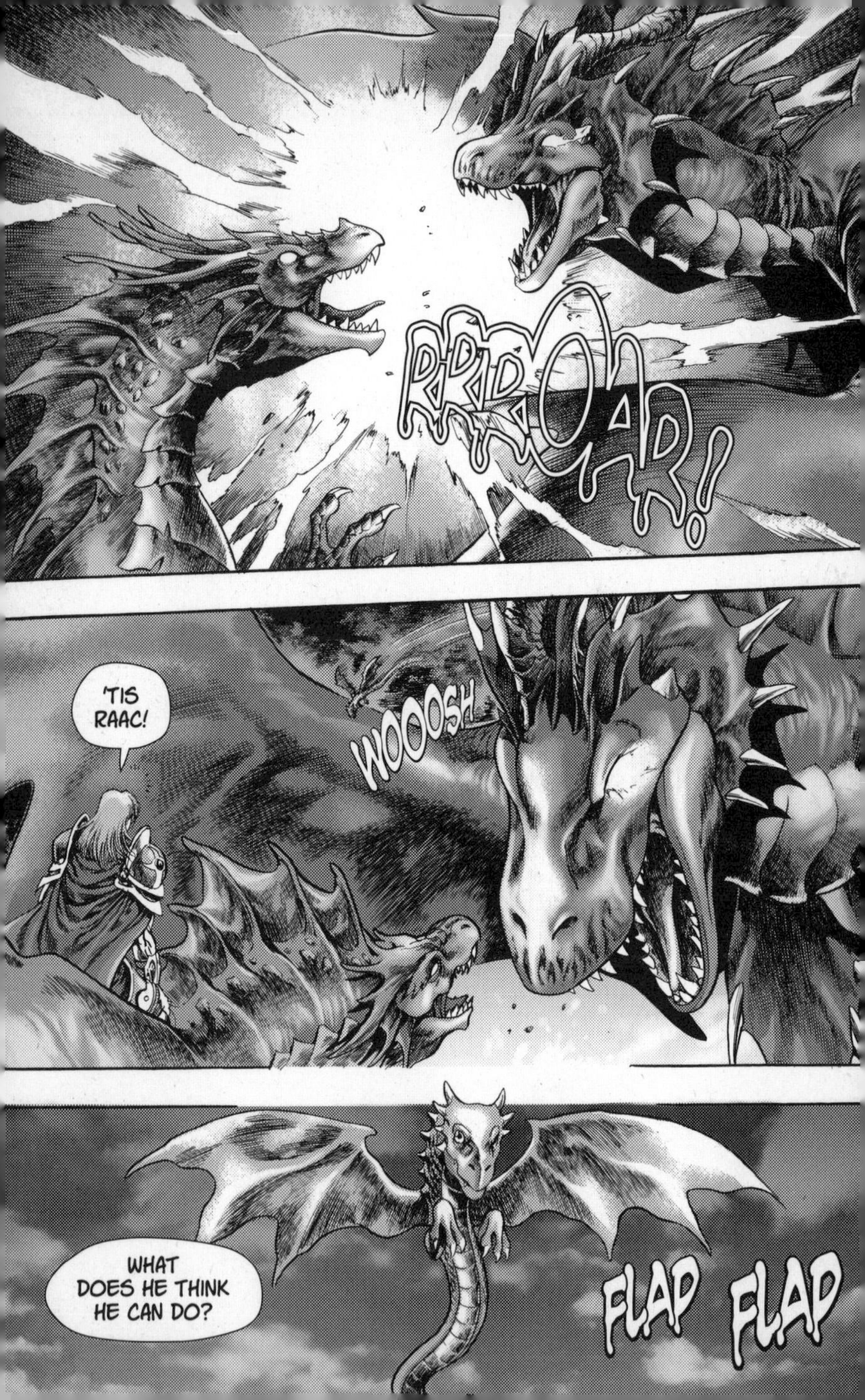
RRRROOAR!
'TIS RAAC!
WOOOSH
WHAT DOES HE THINK HE CAN DO?
FLAP FLAP

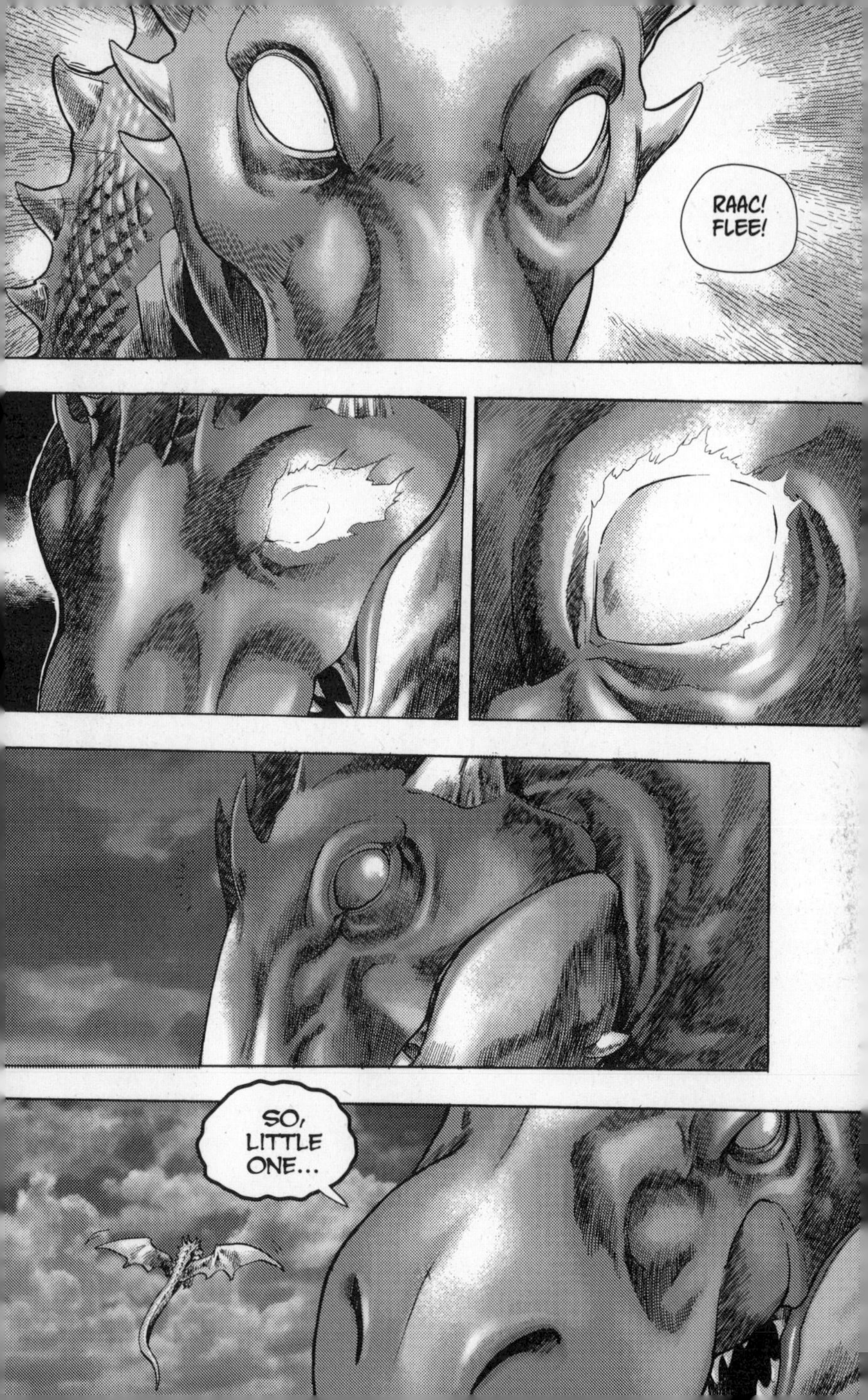
RAAC! FLEE!
SO, LITTLE ONE...

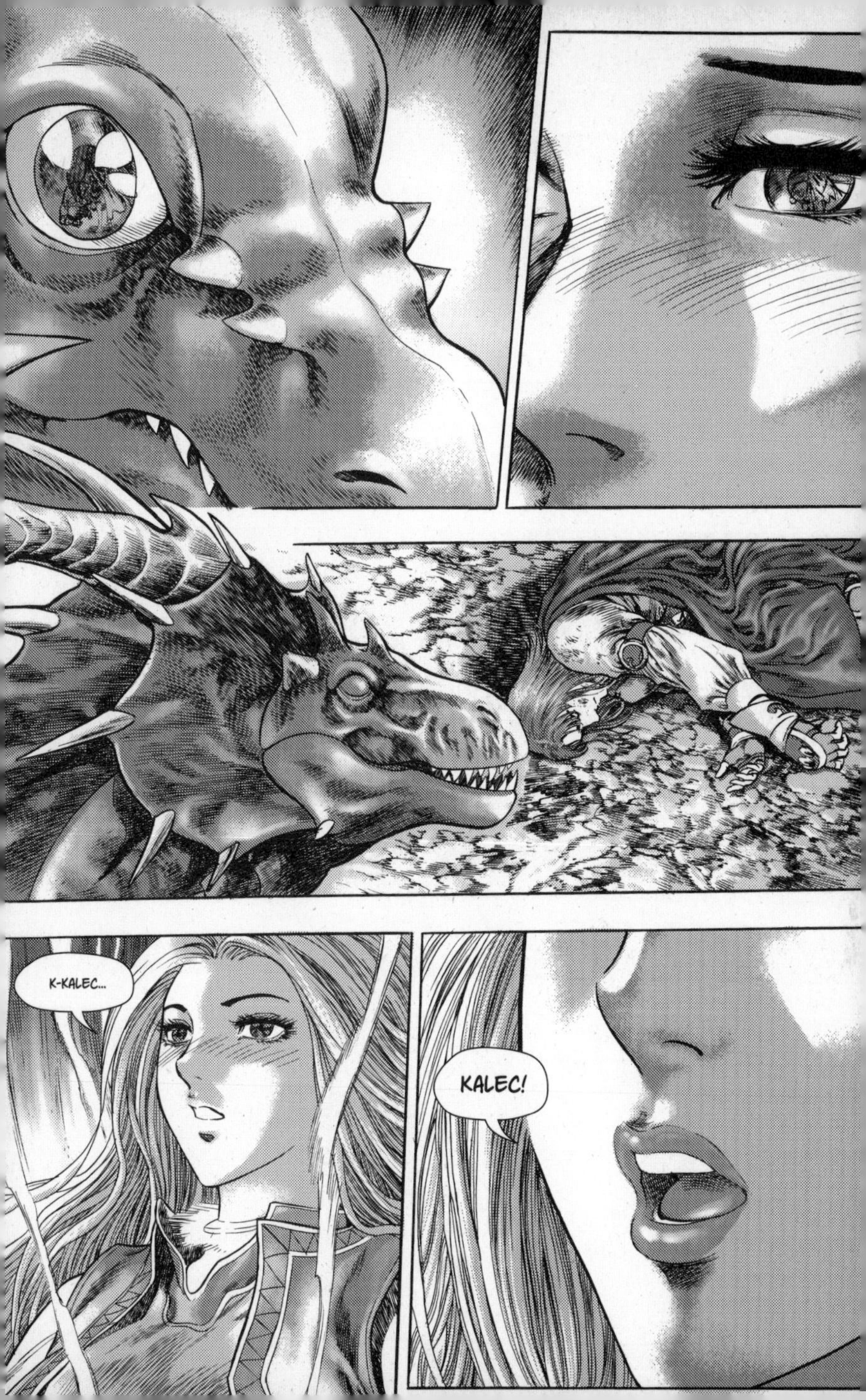
K-KALEC...
KALEC!

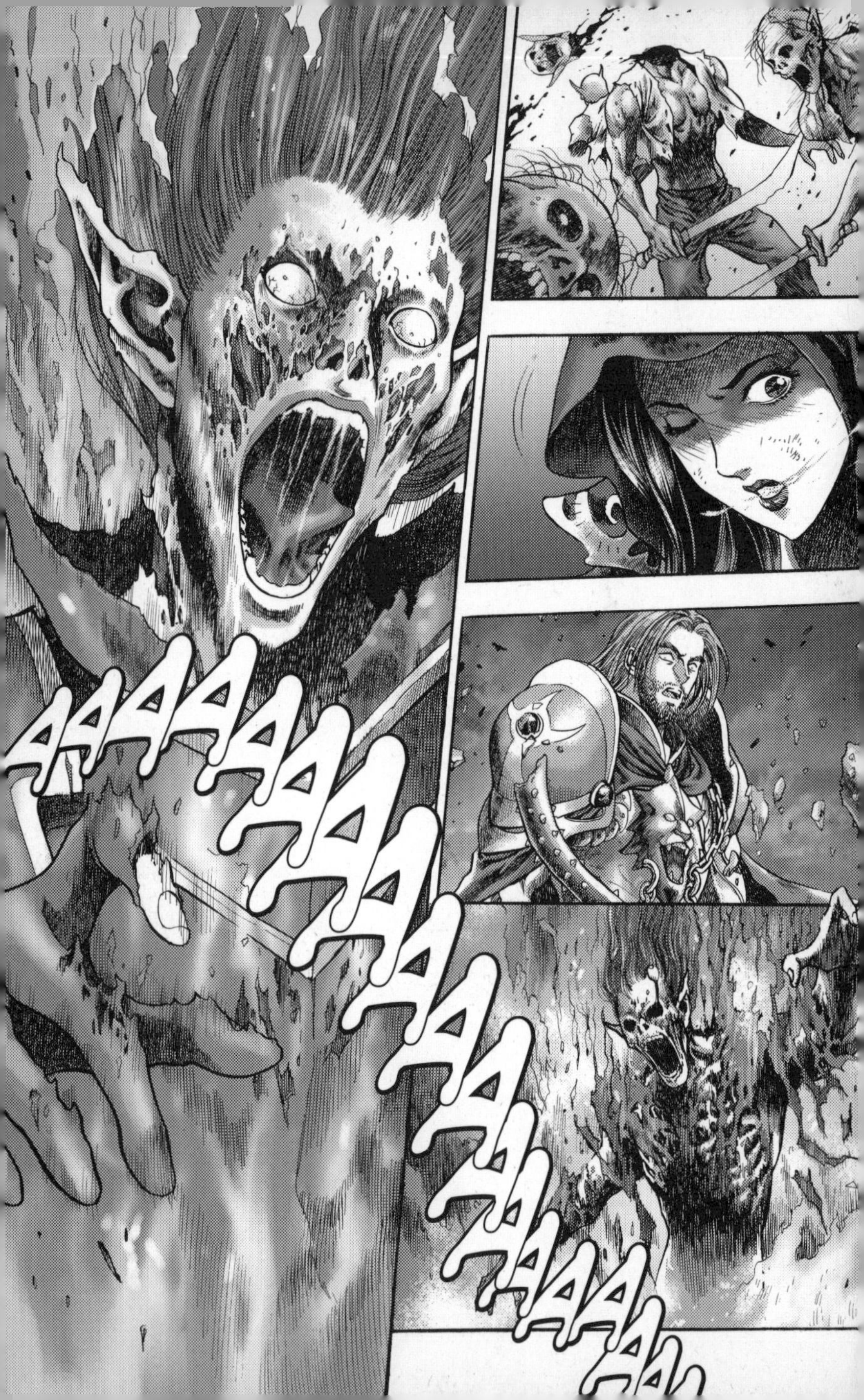
AAAAAAAAAAAAAAAAAAAAAAAAAAAAAA

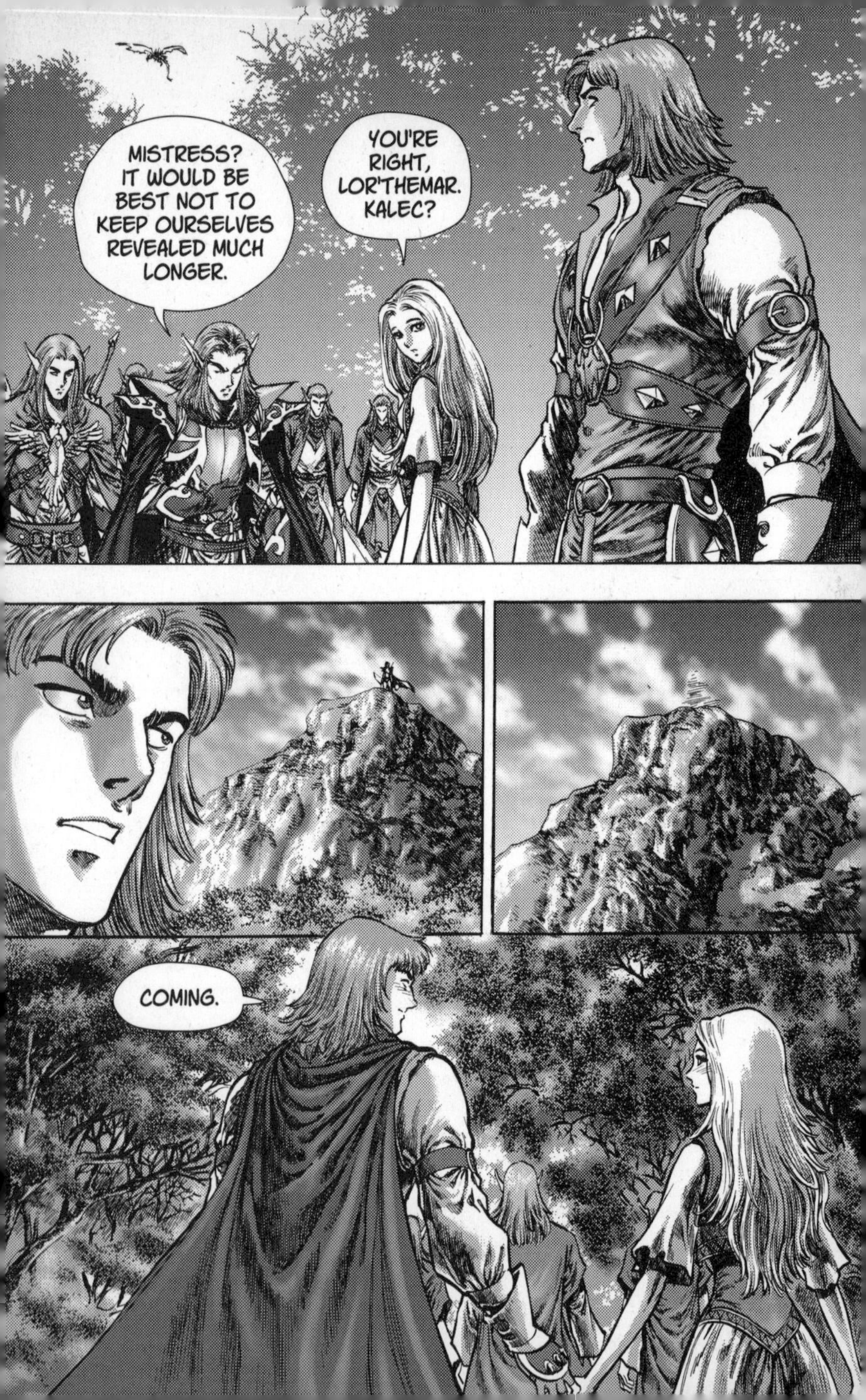
MISTRESS? IT WOULD BE BEST NOT TO KEEP OURSELVES REVEALED MUCH LONGER.
YOU'RE RIGHT, LOR'THEMAR. KALEC?
COMING.

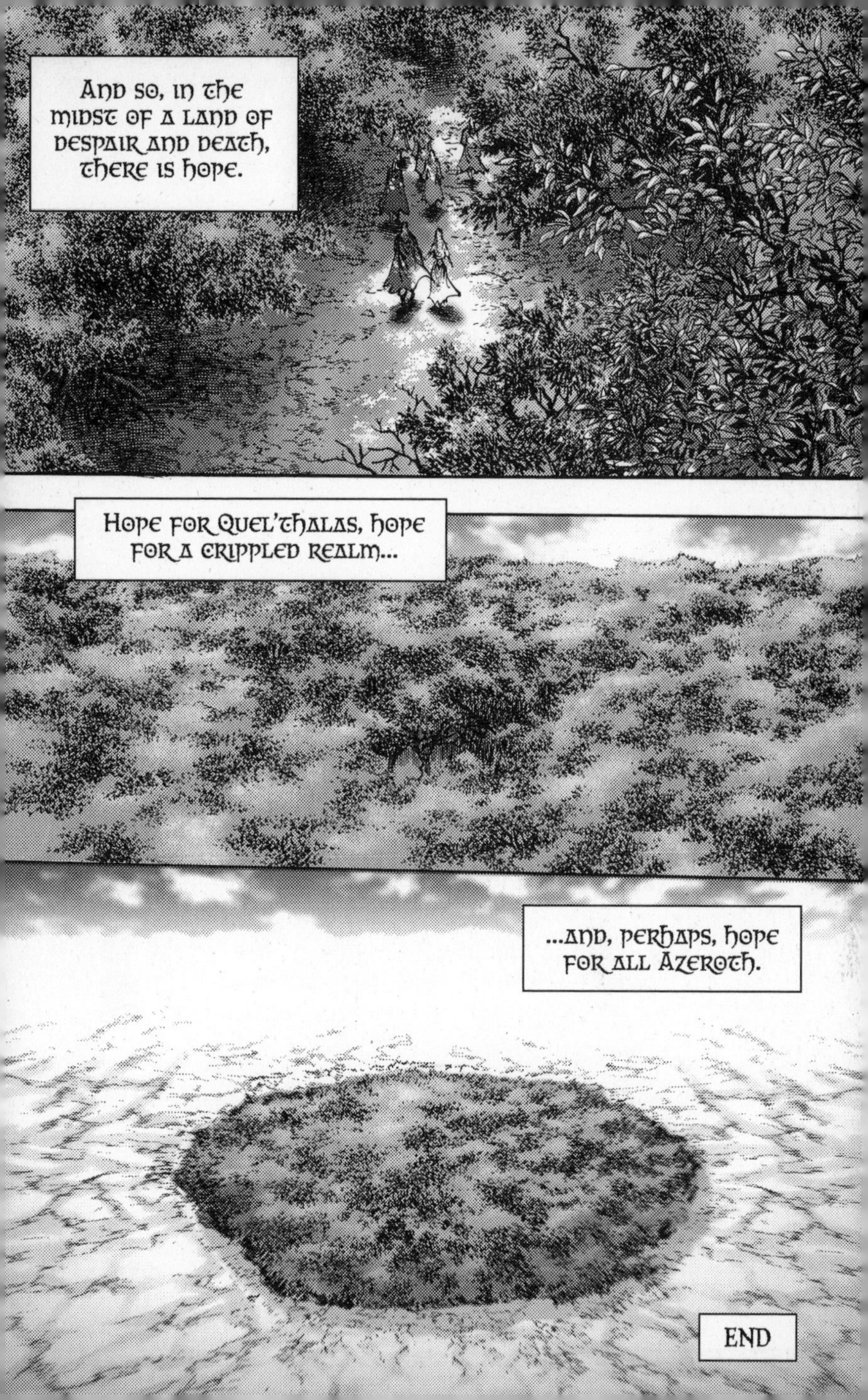
And so, in the midst of a land of despair and death, there is hope.
Hope for Quel'thalas, hope for a crippled realm...
...and, perhaps, hope for all Azeroth.
END

About the

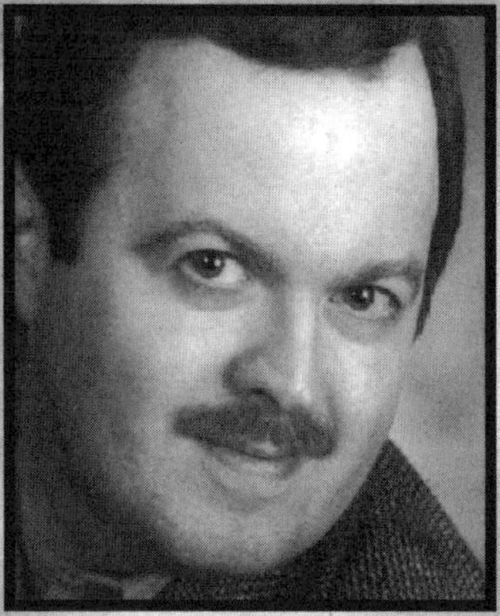

In addition to his work on *Warcraft: The Sunwell Trilogy* and *Ragnarok* (also by TOKYOPOP), Richard A. Knaak is the New York Times bestselling fantasy author of 27 novels and over a dozen short pieces, including *The Legend of Huma* and *Night of Blood* for Dragonlance and *The Demon Soul* for Warcraft. He has also written the popular Dragonrealm series and several independent pieces. His works have been published in several languages, most recently Russian, Turkish, Bulgarian, Chinese, Czech, German, and Spanish.

To find out more about Richard's projects or to join his e-mail list for announcements, visit his website at http://www.sff.net/people/knaak

CREATORS

Jae-Hwan Kim was born in 1971 in Korea. His credits include *Ducal, Combat Metal, Hae Mo Soo, Rainbow, Mech Destroyer, Green Tank Hae Mo Soo TV animation* (produced by KBS), and character designs for *Taengu and Oolashong, Max Man* and an Aerosmith music video.

In addition to *Warcraft: The Sunwell Trilogy*, Jae-Hwan is currently drawing *King Of Hell* and writing and drawing *War Angels*, a fantastic new original series available from TOKYOPOP in July 2007.

Those interested in more information about *Warcraft: The Sunwell Trilogy, King of Hell* or *War Angels* should visit the TOKYOPOP website: www.TOKYOPOP.com.

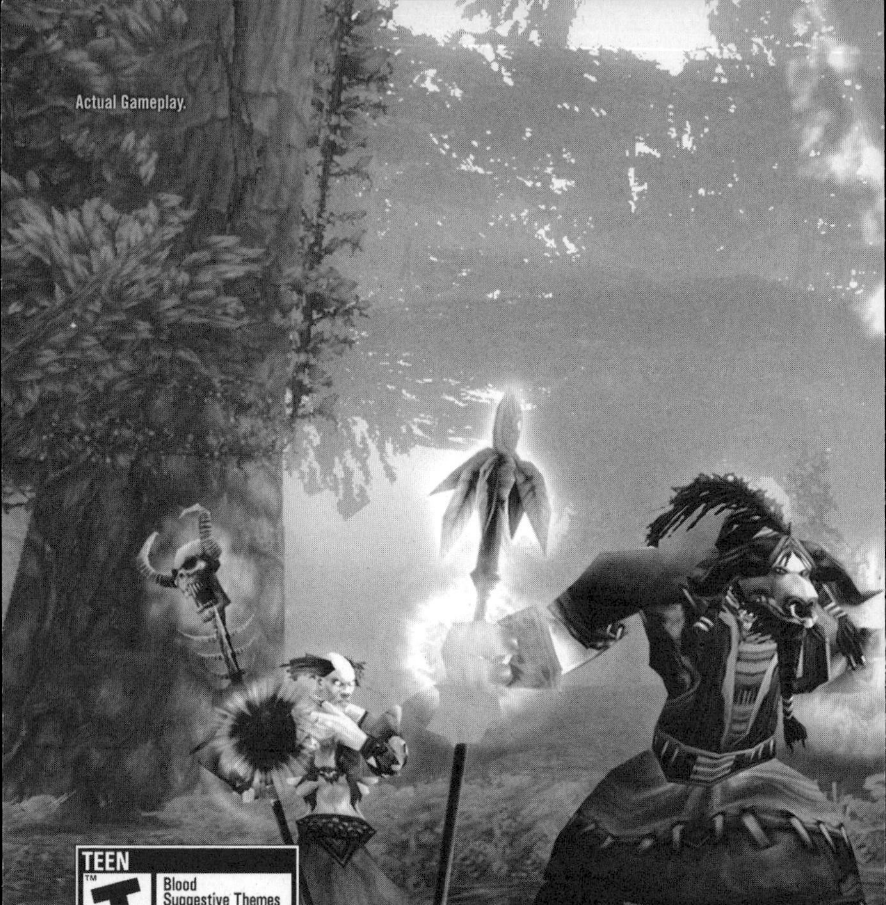
Actual Gameplay.
TEEN
T
Blood
Suggestive Themes
Use of Alcohol
Violence
ESRB CONTENT RATING www.esrb.org
Game Experience May Change During Online Play

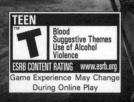

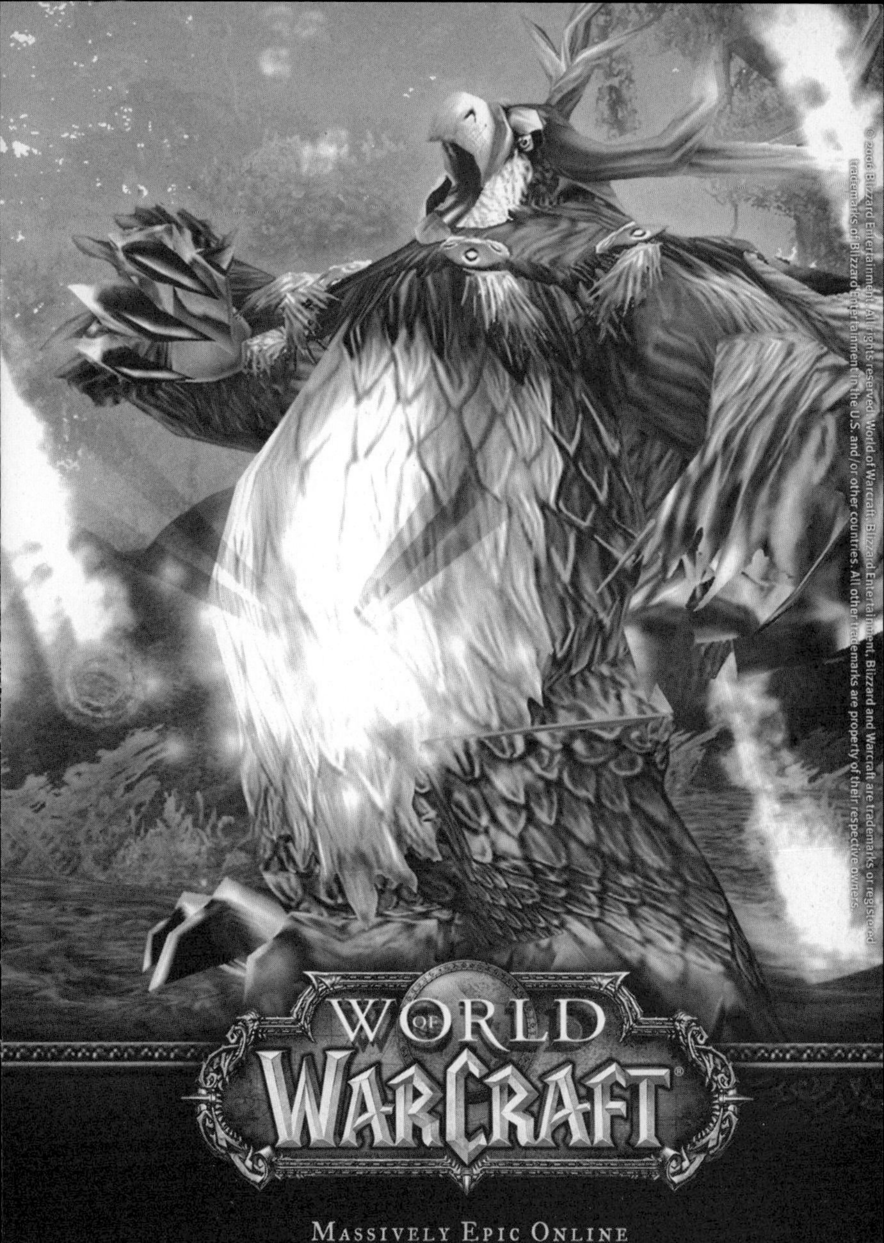
WORLD OF WARCRAFT
MASSIVELY EPIC ONLINE

MAKING YOUR PASSION PORTABLE

WORLD of WARCRAFT
TRADING CARD GAME

DARK PORTAL

◆ Contains brand-new The Burning Crusade™ content including armor, weapons, and the two new races, Blood Elves and Draenei.

◆ Three new Loot™ card items now available! Look for a new blanket, pet or imp companion for your online World of Warcraft™ character.

◆ Supported by extensive Organized Play events such as Release Celebrations, Sneak Previews and exciting Darkmoon Faire tournaments worldwide.

Go to your local hobby store or visit
WWW.UDE.COM/WOW

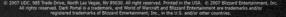

AVAILABLE NOW

WORLD OF WARCRAFT®

RISE OF THE HORDE

BY CHRISTIE GOLDEN

The new novel from Pocket Books
Available wherever books are sold

Also available as an eBook
www.SimonSays.com

TURN THE PAGE FOR A PREVIEW!

M y name is Thrall. The word means "slave" in the human tongue, and the story behind the naming is a long one, best left for another time. By the grace of the spirits and the blood of heroes before me that runs in my veins, I have become Warchief of my people, the orcs, and the leader of a group of races known as the Horde. How this came to be, too, is another tale. The one I wish to set to parchment now, before those who lived it pass to dwell with the honorable ancestors, is the story of my father and those who believed in him; and of those who betrayed him and indeed, all our people.

What might have become of us had these events not unfolded, not even the wise shaman Drek'Thar can say. The paths of Fate are many and varied, and no sane being should ever venture down the deceptively pleasant one of "if only." What happened, happened; my people must shoulder both the shame and the glories of our choices.

This is the tale not of the Horde as it exists today, a loose organization of orc, tauren, forsaken, troll, and blood elf, but of the rise of the very first Horde. Its birth, like that of any infant, was marked by blood and pain, and its harsh cries for life meant death to its enemies.

For such a grim and violent tale, it begins peacefully enough, amid the rolling hills and valleys of a verdant land called Draenor. . . .

The heart-beat rhythm of the drums lulled the younger orcs to sleep, but Durotan of the Frostwolf clan was wide awake. He lay with the others on the hard-packed dirt floor of the sleeping tent. A generous padding of straw and a thick clefthoof pelt protected him from the chill of the bone-cold earth. Even so, he felt the vibrations of the drumming travel up through the earth and into his body, as his ears were caressed by the ancient sound. How he longed to go out and join them!

Durotan would have another summer before he would be able to participate in the *Om'riggor*, the rite of adulthood. Until that much-anticipated event, he would have to accept being shunted off with the children into this large group tent, while the adults sat around the fire and talked of things that were doubtless mysterious and significant.

He sighed and shifted on the pelt. It was not fair.

The orcs did not fight among themselves, but neither were they particularly sociable. Each clan kept to itself, with its own traditions, styles and manner of dress, stories, and shaman. There were even variations of dialect that differed so much that some orcs could not understand one another unless they spoke the common tongue. They almost seemed as different to one another as the other sentient race who shared the bounty of the field, forest, and streams, the blue-skinned, mysterious draenei. Only twice a year, spring and autumn, did all the orc clans come together as they were doing now, to honor that time when day and night were the same length.

The festival had officially started last night at moonrise, though orcs had been gathering at this spot for several days now. The Kosh'harg celebration had been held on this sacred spot in the land the orcs called Nagrand, "Land of Winds," which lay in the benevolent shadow of the "Mountain of Spirits," Oshu'gun, for as long as anyone could remember. While ritual challenges and combat were not unusual during the festival, true anger or violence had never erupted here. When tempers flared, as they sometimes did when so many were gathered together, the shaman encouraged the parties involved to work it out peaceably, or else they were to leave the holy area.

The land in this place was lush and fertile and calming. Durotan sometimes wondered if the land was tranquil because of the willingness of the orcs to bring peace to it, or if the orcs were peaceful because the land was so serene. He often wondered such things, and kept them to himself, for he heard no one else voicing such odd ideas.

Durotan sighed quietly, his thoughts racing, his heart thumping in answering rhythm to the voice of the drums outside. Last night had been wonderful, stirring Durotan's soul. When the Pale Lady cleared the dark line of trees, in Her waning phase but still bright enough to cast a powerful light that was reflected on the blankets of white snow, a cheer had gone up from the throat of every one of the thousands of orcs assembled—wise elders, warriors in their prime, even children held in their mother's strong arms. The wolves, both companions and mounts to the orcs, had joined in with exultant howls. The sound shivered along Durotan's veins as the drumming did now, a deep, primal cry of salutation to the white orb who commanded the night skies. Durotan had glanced around to behold a sea of powerful beings raising their brown hands, silvered in the light, to the Pale Lady, all with one focus. If any ogre had been foolish enough to attack, it would have fallen in a matter of heartbeats beneath the weapons of this vast sea of single-minded warriors.

Then had come feasting. Dozens of beasts had been slain earlier in the season, before the winter had set in, and dried and smoked in preparation for the event. Bonfires had been kindled, their warm light merging with the fey, white glow of the Lady, and the drumming had begun and had not stopped since.

He, like all the other children—lying on his clefthoof pelt, Durotan sniffed dismissively at the term—had been permitted to stay up until he had eaten his fill and the shaman had departed. The shaman of every clan left, once the opening feast had been consumed, to climb Oshu'gun, which stood careful watch over their festivities, enter its caverns, and be advised by the spirits and their ancestors.

Oshu'gun was impressive even from a distance. Unlike other mountains, which were irregular and rough in their shape, Oshu'-gun erupted from the ground with the precision and sharp point of a spearhead. It looked like a giant crystal set into the earth, so clean were its lines and so brightly did it glisten in the sun- and moon-light. Some legends told that it had fallen from the sky hundreds of years ago, and it was so unusual that Durotan thought those tales might be right.

Interesting though Oshu'gun might be, Durotan always thought it a bit unfair that the shaman had to stay there for the entire Kosh'harg festival. The poor shaman, he thought, missed all the fun. But then again, he suspected, so did the children.

During the day, there were hunts and game playing and retelling of the heroics of the ancestors. Each clan had its own stories, and so in addition to the familiar tales Durotan had heard as a youngling, there were new and exciting adventures to listen to.

Entertaining as these were, and as much as Durotan enjoyed them, he burned to know what the adults discussed after the children were drowsing in the sleeping tent, after their bellies were stretched full of good food and pipes had been smoked and various brews had been shared.

He could stand it no longer. Quietly, Durotan sat up, his ears straining for any sounds to indicate that anyone else was awake. He heard nothing, and after a long minute, he got to his feet and began to move slowly toward the entrance.

It was a long, slow progression in the darkened tent. Sleeping children of all ages and sizes were sprawled everywhere in the tent, and one wrong move could awaken them. His heart racing with excitement at his daring, Durotan stepped carefully between the only faintly glimpsed shapes, placing each large foot with the delicacy of the long-legged marsh birds.

It seemed to take an eternity before Durotan finally reached the flap. He stood, trying to calm his breathing, reached out—

And touched a large, smooth-skinned body standing right beside him. He jerked his hand back with a surprised hiss.

"What are you doing?" Durotan whispered.

"What are *you* doing?" the other orc shot back. Abruptly Durotan grinned at how foolish they sounded.

"Same thing you are," Durotan replied, his voice still soft. All about them, the others slept on. "We can either keep talking about it or do it."

Durotan could tell by the size of the faint shape in front of him that the orc was a large male, probably close to his own age. He couldn't place the scent or the voice, so it wasn't one of the Frostwolf clan. It was a daring thought—not only to do something so forbidden as to leave the sleeping tent without permission, but to do so in the company of an orc not of his own clan.

The other orc hesitated, the same thoughts no doubt running through his head. "Very well," he said at last. "Let's do it."

Durotan reached out again in the darkness, his fingers brushing the hide of the flap and curling around its edge. The two orc youths pulled back the flap and stepped out into the frosty night.

Durotan turned to look at his companion. The other orc was brawnier than he, and stood a bit taller. Durotan was the largest of his age in his clan, and unused to others being taller than he. It was a bit disquieting. His ally in mischief turned to look at him, and Durotan felt himself being assessed. The other nodded, apparently satisfied with what he saw.

They did not risk words. Durotan pointed to a large tree close to the tent, and silently the two headed for it. For a moment that was probably not as long as it felt, they were in the open, exposed to any adult who chose that instant to turn his head and see them, but they were not spotted. Durotan felt as exposed as if he were in bright sunlight, so powerful was the moon's glow reflected off the crystalline snow. And surely the sound of the snow squeaking beneath their feet was as loud as the bellow of an enraged ogre. At last they reached the tree and sank down behind it. Durotan's breath misted as he finally exhaled. The other orc turned to him and grinned.

"I am Orgrim, line of Telkar Doomhammer, of the Blackrock clan," the youth said in a proud whisper.

Durotan was impressed. While the Doomhammer line was not the line of a chieftain, it was well known and honored.

"I am Durotan, line of Garad, of the Frostwolf clan," Durotan replied. Now it was Orgrim's turn to react to the fact that he was sitting with the heir to another clan. He nodded approvingly.

For a moment they simply sat, reveling in the glory of their daring. Durotan began to feel the cold and wetness seep through his thick hide cape, and got to his feet. Again, he pointed at the gathering, and Orgrim nodded. They carefully peered around the tree, straining to listen. Surely now they would hear the mysteries for which they both hungered. Over the crackling sound of the huge bonfire and the deep, steady beating of the drums, voices floated to them.

"The shaman have been kept busy this winter with the fever," Durotan's father, Garad, said. He reached down and petted the huge white wolf who was drowsing by the fire. The beast, its white coat distinguishing it as a Frostwolf, made a soft crooning sound of pleasure. "Soon as one of the younglings gets cured, another falls ill."

"I am ready for spring, myself," another male said, standing and tossing another log on the fire. "It's been harsh with the animals, too. When we were preparing for the festival, we had a hard time finding clefthooves."

"Klaga makes a delicious soup from the bones, but she refuses to tell us what herbs she uses," a third said, glaring at a female who was nursing an infant. The female in question, presumably Klaga, chuckled.

"The only one who'll get that recipe is this little one when she comes of age," Klaga replied, and grinned.

Durotan's jaw dropped. He turned his head to stare at Orgrim, who wore a similar expression of stunned dismay. *This* was what was so important, so secret that the children were forbidden to leave the tent to listen to it? Discussions of fevers and soups?

In the bright light of the moon, Durotan had no trouble seeing Orgrim's face clearly. The other youth's brows drew together in a frown.

"You and I can come up with something more interesting than this, Durotan," he said in a low, gruff voice.

Durotan grinned and nodded. He was certain of it.

⋆　⋆　⋆

The festival lasted for two more days. During the daytime and at night, when the two would sneak out together, they challenged each other to different contests of skill. Racing, climbing, strength, sure-footedness—everything they could think of. And each defeated the other almost as if they had planned on taking turns. When, on the last day, Orgrim loudly called for a fifth challenge to break the stalemate, something inside Durotan made him speak.

"Let us not perform common, ordinary challenges," Durotan said, wondering where the words came from even as he uttered them. "Let us do something truly different in the history of our people."

Orgrim's bright gray eyes gleamed as he leaned forward. "What do you suggest?"

"Let us be friends, you and I."

Orgrim's heavily muscled jaw dropped. "But—we are not of the same clan!" he said, in a voice that indicated that Durotan might have proposed a friendship between the great black wolf and the mild talbuk.

Durotan waved a dismissive hand. "We are not enemies," he said. "Look around you. The clans come together twice a year and there is no harm in it."

"But . . . my father says it is precisely *because* we come together so seldom that the peace is kept," Orgrim continued. His brow knotted with concern.

Disappointment colored Durotan's words with bitterness. "Very well. I thought you braver than the others, Orgrim of the Doomhammer line, but you are no better than they—timid and shy and unwilling to see beyond what has always been done to what is possible."

The words had come from his heart, but had Durotan calculated them and honed them for weeks, he could not have chosen better. Orgrim's brown face flushed and his eyes snapped.

"I am no coward!" he snarled. "I back down from no challenge, you upstart Frostwolf!"

He sprang on Durotan then, knocking the smaller orc off his feet, and the two pummeled each other until the shaman needed to be brought in for healing and lecturing on the inappropriateness of fighting in a sacred space.

"Impetuous boy," scolded the head shaman of the Frostwolves, an ancient orc female they called "Mother" Kashur. "You are not too old to be beaten as a disobedient child, young Durotan!"

The shaman who tended Orgrim muttered similar displeased sounds. But even as blood streamed freely from his nose, and as he watched the shaman heal a wicked gash on Orgrim's brown torso, Durotan grinned. Orgrim caught his gaze and grinned back.

The challenge had begun, the final challenge, so much more important than races or lifting stones, and neither was willing to admit defeat . . . to say that a friendship between two youths of different clans was wrong. Durotan had a feeling that this particular challenge would end only when one of them was dead . . . and perhaps not even then.

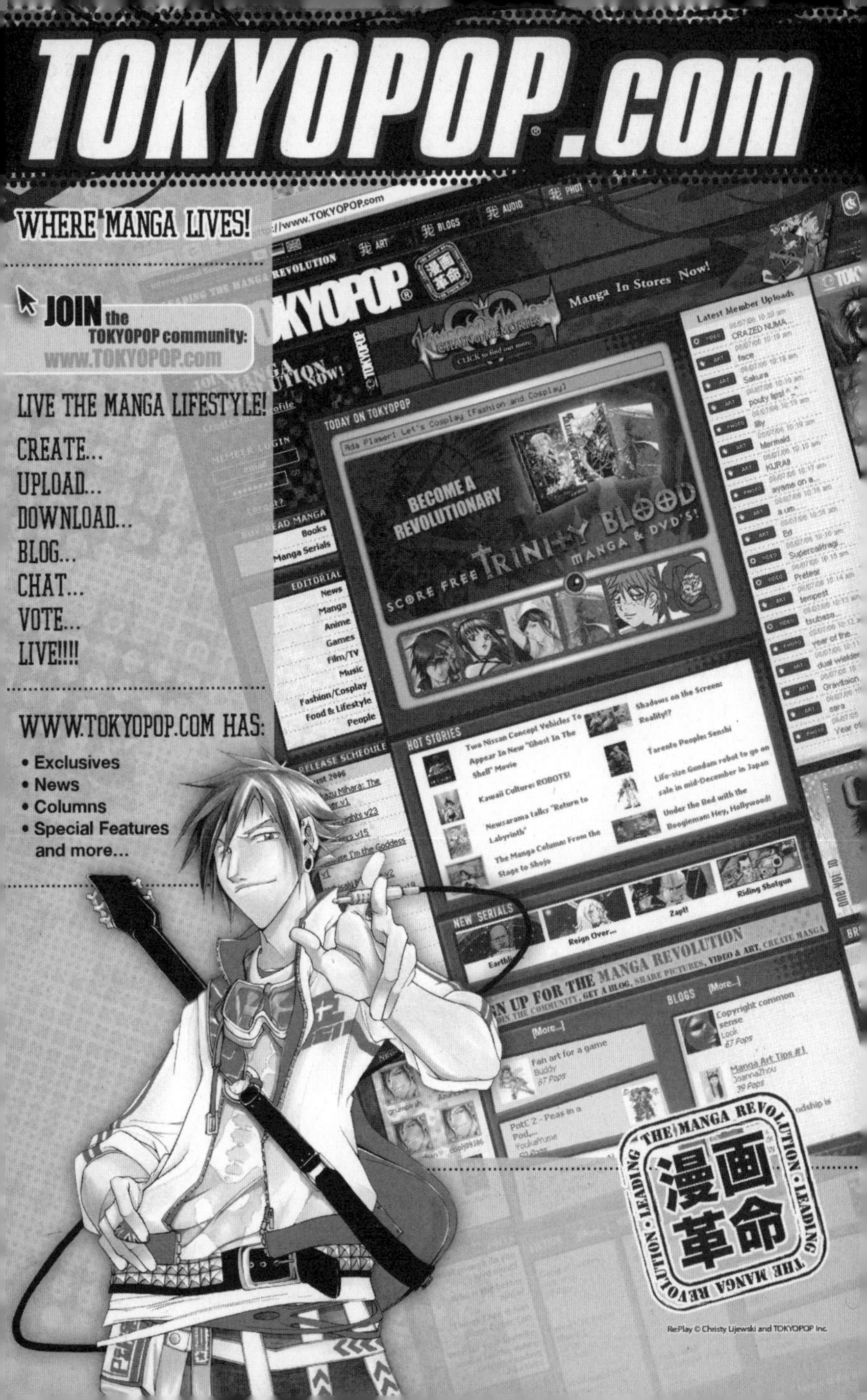
TOKYOPOP.com
WHERE MANGA LIVES!
JOIN the TOKYOPOP community:
www.TOKYOPOP.com
LIVE THE MANGA LIFESTYLE!
CREATE...
UPLOAD...
DOWNLOAD...
BLOG...
CHAT...
VOTE...
LIVE!!!!
WWW.TOKYOPOP.COM HAS:
• Exclusives
• News
• Columns
• Special Features and more...
THE MANGA REVOLUTION • LEADING
漫画革命
Re:Play © Christy Lijewski and TOKYOPOP Inc.

The DARK GOODBYE
A HARDBOILED NOIR SUSPENSE THRILLER GUARANTEED TO LEAVE YOU DEAD!
FROM THE TWISTED MIND OF FRANK MARRAFFINO!
ART BY DREW RAUSCH, CREATOR OF SULLENGREY!
Hired to locate a missing girl, Detective Max "Mutt" Mason discovers deeper malignant forces at work. Femmes fatale soon give way to strange creatures older than humanity, all bent on remaking our world as their own. Mason has questions, but is he ready for the answers?
HORROR
OT
OLDER TEEN AGE 16+
©2007 Frank Marraffino and TOKYOPOP Inc.

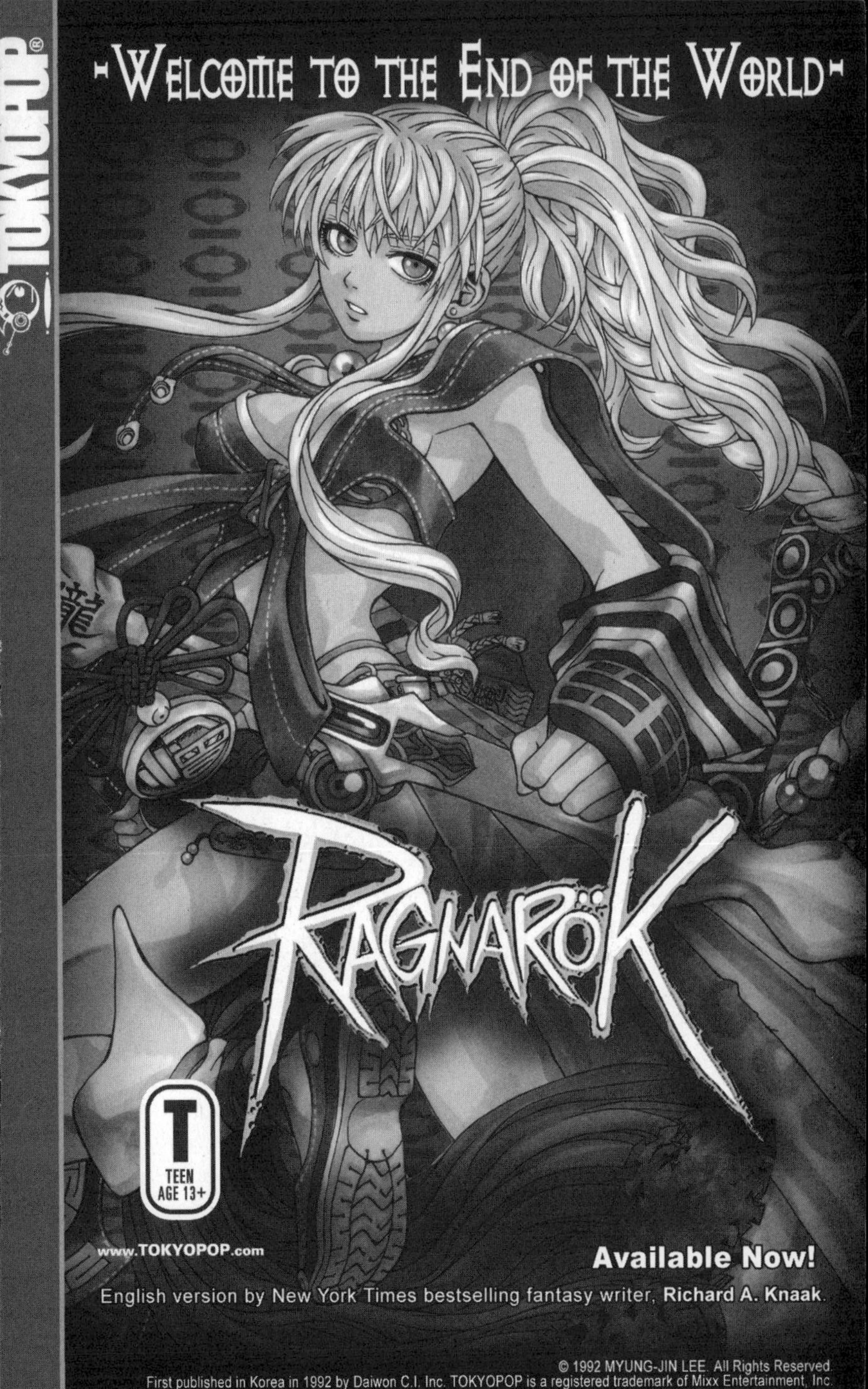
TOKYOPOP
-WELCOME TO THE END OF THE WORLD-
RAGNARÖK
T
TEEN
AGE 13+
www.TOKYOPOP.com
Available Now!
English version by New York Times bestselling fantasy writer, Richard A. Knaak.
© 1992 MYUNG-JIN LEE. All Rights Reserved.
First published in Korea in 1992 by Daiwon C.I. Inc. TOKYOPOP is a registered trademark of Mixx Entertainment, Inc.

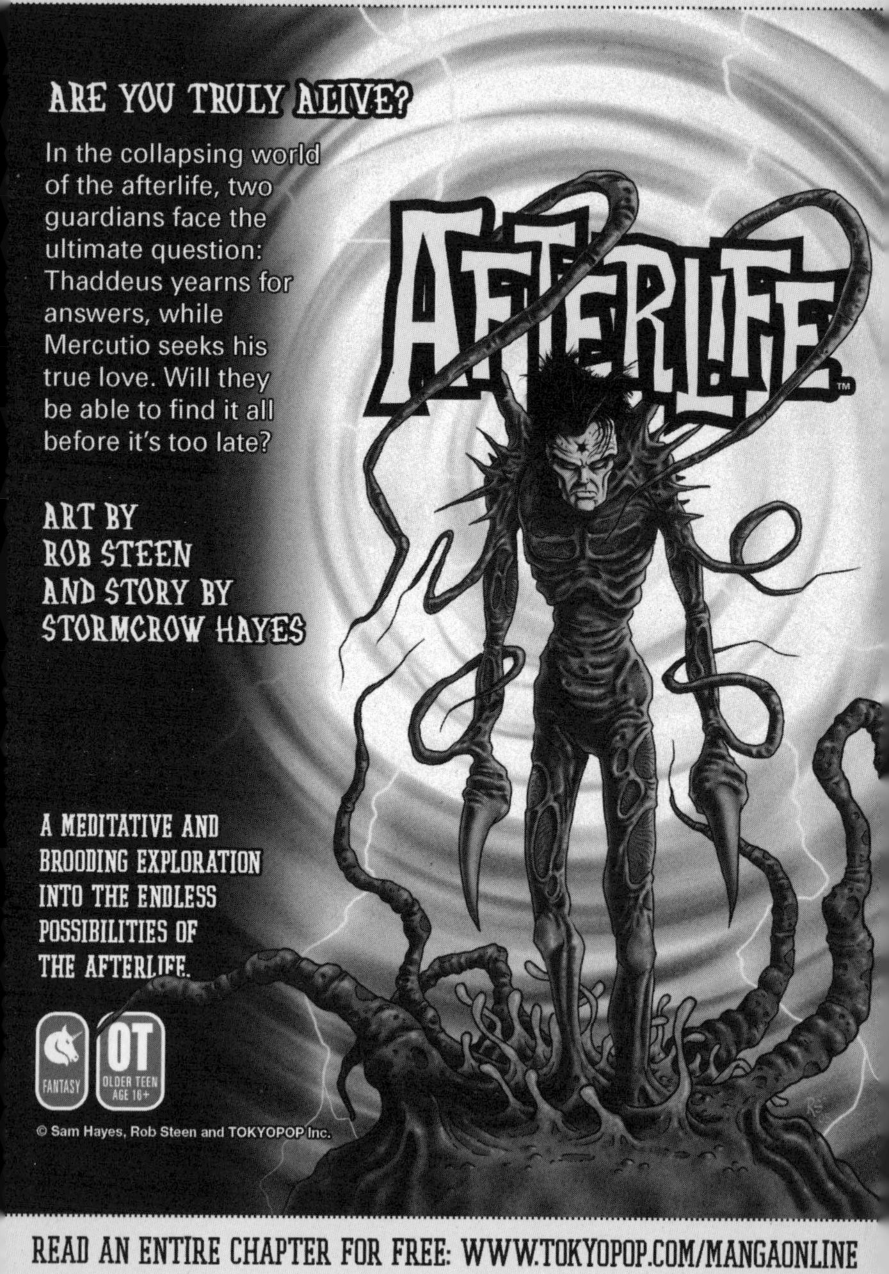
ARE YOU TRULY ALIVE?
In the collapsing world of the afterlife, two guardians face the ultimate question: Thaddeus yearns for answers, while Mercutio seeks his true love. Will they be able to find it all before it's too late?
AFTERLIFE™
ART BY ROB STEEN AND STORY BY STORMCROW HAYES
A MEDITATIVE AND BROODING EXPLORATION INTO THE ENDLESS POSSIBILITIES OF THE AFTERLIFE.
FANTASY
OT
OLDER TEEN AGE 16+
© Sam Hayes, Rob Steen and TOKYOPOP Inc.